The Real Me

The Real Me

Find and Express Your Authentic Self

Mark Eyre

BEP BUSINESS EXPERT PRESS

First published in 2017 by
Business Expert Press, LLC
222 East 46th Street, New York, NY 10017
www.businessexpertpress.com

ISBN-13: 978-1-63157-703-1 (paperback)
ISBN-13: 978-1-63157-704-8 (e-book)

Business Expert Press Human Resource Management and
Organizational Behavior Collection

Collection ISSN: 1946-5637 (print)
Collection ISSN: 1946-5645 (electronic)

Cover and interior design by S4Carlisle Publishing Services
Private Ltd., Chennai, India

First edition: 2017

10 9 8 7 6 5 4 3 2 1

Printed in the United States of America.

Abstract

Modern society is ill. Many people sit in their work cubicle, in jobs that are stressful and unfulfilling. With a boss they don't like. With a mortgage they cannot afford. With relationships that aren't all they could be. With a work-life balance that's all work and no life. It's no wonder there's a stress and depression epidemic in the Western world. Many people have simply lost themselves.

Is this you? If so, life doesn't have to be like this. You can choose to live life in a different way.

Most people will say that they want more than anything to be themselves and to make a difference. This book is about how to be true to yourself in a society that more than ever pushes us to disguise who we are, so we end up pretending to be who we're not.

How can I find a way to be myself? Join Mark Eyre to find your own *real me*, and along the way, pick up some practical strategies and approaches to help you express who you really are. It's time to join the journey of a lifetime, and in the words of George Eliot, to "be who you might have been."

Keywords

Authenticity, personal leadership, well-being, influencing, self-esteem, personal development, personal identity, self-help, assertiveness, self-belief, self-expression.

Contents

List of Figures

TABLES

Introduction

The privilege of a lifetime is to become who you truly are
—Carl Gustav Jung

A few years ago, my family and I moved house after the birth of our second child. This allowed us the opportunity to clear out the attic, and rifle through old boxes that we never look at the rest of the time.

In three such boxes were my old photo albums, from my precomputer days of taking photos. I spent a couple of hours going through them, ostensibly to clear them out. However, looking through my old photographs again stirred long forgotten memories. Pictures of me at school, with my family, as a teenager, and my graduation photos. Photos of me with friends at work, on holidays, forming a kaleidoscope of my life through its many different phases. This clearing out exercise left me with plenty to reflect on.

By now, you might be thinking of your old photographs. Some of your photos you will remember vividly in your mind's eye, and many more you may have forgotten about. I'd like you to imagine going through your old pictures and videos, recording the key stages of your life. Your photos with family, friends, first love, partners, at school, work and on holidays, when you became a parent, and perhaps even when your kids left home. As you look back, you will remember good times, happy times, bad and sad times in your life. What kind of person were you at these different times? How did you think and act at each stage of your life? Did you stay essentially the same, or did you change? If you behaved differently, what was it that caused this? Did you make a conscious decision to behave differently?

Having reminisced a bit, now bring your mind back to the present. Imagine a typical day in your life as it is now. You will spend time with your family and friends, at work, dealing with professional colleagues and customers, seniors and juniors, and other people you just meet in the day, from ticket collectors to shop assistants. Is your behavior consistent, or does it vary during the day with different people and in different situations? If all the people you met were to describe you, would they be describing the same person? Would you find yourself saying things like *no, that's not what I'm really like*? Many of us find that, as we move between situations, we unconsciously assume a different mask, being a different person in each case. This means that we are, to some degree, at least hiding who we really are from other people, and maybe from ourselves too.

Who is this book for?

Many people in modern life face an unparalleled crisis of identity. The classic questions of *who am I*, and *why am I here?* have never seemed to matter so much. Many people right now are sitting in their lives wondering what it's all about. They are sat in a job they don't like, with a boss they don't respect, and no sense that their career is going anywhere interesting. They face escalating costs, high mortgages, and thanks to a near decade of austerity, they can see no way to ease the pressure. They are stuck in marriages that are no longer working in the way they once hoped, surrounded by family and other pressures. Pressure, pressure, pressure!

My book is for those who sit wondering what happened to their life, and why it can't be better. If you think that the Scott Adams creation *Dilbert* sums working life up, then this book is for you. Career centered but frustrated, recognizing that there is an outside life (or should be), and fed up with putting on an act for other people. You have realized that it's time for the acting to end, and for life to begin.

Why am I writing this book?

I am writing this book because I believe many of us have lost sight of who we really are, the *real me*. Who you were when you arrived on this planet has adapted in many different ways as you move through the stages of life. However, you can spend so much time adapting that you lose yourself in the process. Instead, you become a succession of acts, behaving differently in different parts of your life. The result is that you end up not living your own life at all; it doesn't feel like it anyway.

We gradually accumulate a wardrobe full of masks for different occasions. We have a work mask and a domestic mask. We might also have a mask for our family and key relationships, and a different one for our friends. In fact, we may have a different mask for all the organizations and networks we're part of. Depending on our sex, we may have other masks to wear. For example, the *stiff upper lip* or *grin and bear it* mask that many men are required to wear, the logical extension of the childhood lesson many are taught—*big boys don't cry*. In contrast, many women are raised with the lesson that it's not OK to be angry. Hence the maxim that upset men shout, and angry women cry. Finally, we have a big society mask we wear at times, the *good citizen* mask for example.

In modern life, we are submerged under masks of different sorts. But who is the *real me*? Following the approaches in this book will enable you to become better connected with your own *real me*, so your life will feel like your own.

My own journey has been one of self-discovery, or self-rediscovery to be more accurate. I lost myself in childhood, amid a welter of changes that moved me away from being the real me. I learned to put on a variety of masks in different situations to gain acceptance from others. That continued into my academic life, and during the time I entered the world of work, and large corporations.

For 25 years, I was gainfully employed in corporate life. I realized that I had a passion for helping people to develop themselves. However, I allowed myself to be ground down by organizational life and other people's expectations. I felt uncomfortable being asked to do things I didn't believe in. I felt even more uncomfortable with being asked to say things I didn't believe in! I got fed up with the politics and manipulation, and frustrated with myself for keeping quiet and playing the game.

In the end, I did what many people do, and sat in my office cubicle wondering what my life had come to, why it didn't feel good, and why I never felt in control of anything that really mattered. In the end, it came down to a choice between becoming cynical, disillusioned and sarcastic (all of which I could do!), or doing something about it. I chose the latter course, and embarked on a journey to find my own *real me*. I now run my own business, dedicated to helping people become all they can be. I have always had an interest in empowerment, helping people to empower themselves to take responsibility for their own work and lives.

As I look back on my life, and the lives I see around me, I see a play. In this play, there are millions of actors and actresses on a literally global stage. They are all playing a variety of roles, just as we are. Whether we are empowered or not, we act out a variety of roles in life. The consequences of all this include personal crises, depression, stress, and collapsed personal relationships. All of these problems are at historically epidemic levels.

The medical profession has identified a range of modern diseases that are now epidemic in the advanced world, including stress, depression, diabetes and obesity. Professor Phil Hanlon [1] was, until recently, the Professor of Public Health at the University of Glasgow. He pointed out that these modern diseases were no longer controllable using the same medical models that cured the diseases of the 18th, 19th and early 20th centuries. With modern illnesses, it's proving much more difficult to understand the causes, and therefore less easy to control in the way past illnesses were. What has created this epidemic of modern diseases?

I believe the loss of personal coherence, or understanding of our own true identity, is one reason we face this epidemic which is ruining the lives of many in our communities. It is not without accident that the word *disease* can be broken down into *dis-ease*. It is the lack of ease many people feel with modern life that has given rise to these modern diseases.

For most people, the major motivation for seeking change is to ease or escape from something that is painful to them. As the Chinese recognized thousands of years ago, a crisis situation also presents us with an opportunity to do something about it, should we choose to do so. The pain faced by many people is heavily influenced by the nature of the society we live in. Our societies, and leaders within them, increasingly channel much of our attention in such a way as to generate fear, whether they are conscious of doing so or not. Matters like recession, wars, tragedies, disasters, and general foreboding don't provide a foundation for feeling good. It should come as no surprise that in our day-to-day lives, we spend more time worrying than hoping. This does not help in our search for a better life.

The era in which we live is widely viewed as one of global transformation. Looking at the current economic climate and rising global protests, there is convincing evidence that in some ways, things may never be the same again. The game of *work hard and you'll make money and get a good pension* is now exposed as a facade. If people don't know yet what they want, there is ample evidence that they are becoming clearer about what it is they don't want.

A strong grasp on our own identity is vital when faced with a difficult or uncertain future. Viktor Frankl famously wrote about *Man's search for meaning* [2], and I believe that one key to finding greater meaning in our lives is to find better ways to *get real*. The issue of who we are has been around for centuries. Just under 400 years ago, Rene Descartes [3] pursued just this topic with his now famous observation, often condensed into *I think therefore I am*:

> After considering everything very thoroughly, I must finally conclude that this proposition, I *am*, I *exist,* is necessarily true whenever it is put forward by me or conceived in my mind. (Descartes et al., 1984)

The concept of personal identity is not new. But the modern challenges to it with our postindustrial society undoubtedly are. The result is that we search for substitutes to bring in an identikit identity—putting on masks at work, following fashions, and even putting an identity together on Facebook. We search for spiritual meaning, we look at our family history, and we try many different strategies, all to find substance to our own identity.

However, it is the search for our core self that is the key to truly finding the *real me*. This book is about how we find this connection. Understanding the ways that we become disconnected from ourselves is the first step to salvation. From there, we will move on to building, or rebuilding, our own level of personal coherence—becoming more of a whole person, based around the *real me*. We will illustrate this with examples of masked and unmasked responses in different situations, so you can see what they look like.

To those among you who may be thinking of how difficult it is to change yourself, I would say that I am not urging you to change yourself. I am urging you to find yourself again, and that is a different thing entirely.

In making this transition, we will echo Paolo Coelho's [4] famous journey depicted in *The Alchemist*, where a boy from Spain set off for the African desert and the Egyptian pyramids in his search for treasure. In the story, it was only at the end that the boy learned that the true treasure was at home, right where he'd come from. This parallels our own personal journey, looking outside for inspiration, when true inspiration comes from within us, by finding who we really are and then projecting it. I am inviting you in this book to become more self-consciously individual, and perhaps to become less conformist.

Be yourself is one piece of advice I've heard many times, but before you can be it, you have to find it. As you do find it, you will reclaim your place in the world, the one you were born for.

Mark Eyre—September 30, 2016

PART 1

The Legacy of Incoherence

CHAPTER 1

Coherent Death, Incoherent Life

You don't get to choose how you're going to die, only how you're going to live

—Joan Baez

Begin with the end in mind is great advice. One thing I've always tried to bear in mind is the one thing most of us cheerfully go around trying to ignore. But ignoring it is futile, because we know the day will eventually arrive. One day, we are going to die. Against this background, one question I've always toyed with when making key life decisions is this: What do you want your own epitaph to say about you?

Given this philosophy, imagine my unbounded joy when I attended a management seminar a few years ago, near the start of what became my own personal development journey. The speaker was a thoroughly engaging man called Richard Leider [1]. He cited as part of his presentation a study conducted into the elderly, with a cross section of them being asked one question. The question was, "What advice would you give to younger people on how they should live their life based on your own experience?"

Their answers have since been reinforced by further survey material I've seen, and there are a few core themes. These themes are as follows:

1. Be more reflective about life, don't run around so much. It's not worth worrying about things that won't matter in a year or two's time. So, take time out to relax and do what you enjoy.

2. Have courage to be yourself. Where you don't do this, you will live to regret it. Don't be a poor impersonator of someone else when you can be a first class yourself.

3. Get clear about your purpose, why you're here. Why do you get up in the morning? Find out what contribution it is that you want to make.

4. Take the chance! Most people don't regret at the end of their lives the things they did. They regret what they didn't do, or didn't try.

5. Tell those around you how you really feel. That goes both for those you are close to, but also for those situations where you are annoyed or irritated with someone. Burying those feelings does you no good, and does no one else any good either.

✳

What struck me at the time I first heard this was how much the advice had to do with authenticity: That being authentic, or true to ourselves, is vital to living a more fulfilled life. But being authentic depends on our own personal coherence, which is our own sense of who we really are, the *real me*.

People with a coherent view of their own identity know who they naturally are, and if they have to adapt in certain situations, they are aware of this. They are clear that they are compromising, and what they are compromising. In contrast, incoherent, fragmented people have lost touch with who they really are, and may not realize just what they are compromising anymore. We've all met personalities who appear to behave naturally, and seem at ease with themselves. It is personal coherence that helps them to be like this.

The importance of being ourselves in life has been reinforced by Bronnie Ware [2], a palliative care nurse who cared for people in the last few weeks of their lives. She made notes of the top regrets her patients expressed to her. There should be no prizes for working out the top regret: It was as follows:

I wish I'd had the courage to live a life true to myself, not the life others expected of me. (Ware, 2012)

Our personal coherence or lack thereof, underpins all of this. Reforming ourselves is therefore a key step to regaining our own purpose, and moving toward a life we really want. We literally need to pull ourselves together if we want that better life. The irony is that we are born personally coherent. Babies live life true to themselves. We didn't put on an act when we were that young. But, for many of us, we learned how not to be ourselves as we grew up. We need to relearn how to do this.

An Incoherent Act

We all play different roles at different times, donning different masks. We take on a role in our job, and often our work behavior is different from our behavior at home, with our partner and family, with our friends. We may behave differently again in social organizations that we might be members of, with their codes of conduct and expectations of how we should behave.

It is desirable to behave differently sometimes. I would not recommend that we discard all sense of convention, restraint and obligation in our behavior. As civilization progressed, it was necessary to develop and evolve rules of behavior, and other societal constraints. Indeed, without them, we do not have a civilization to speak of! I would argue though that we have developed these rules too far, and in too many areas, for them to be healthy anymore. We live in a society that is increasingly preoccupied with the concept of identity. Even campaigns to introduce identity cards presuppose that we have a personal identity—why, we may even have it stolen from us by online thieves. Terrorists are becoming more adept at forging or creating false passports, giving themselves a new identity. We look all around us, and all we can see is identity.

This focus on identity conceals the fact that many people have lost touch with who they really are. The very trouble with identities is precisely that they can be created in the first place, as the many celebrities who reinvent themselves regularly demonstrate. Anthony Robbins [3] defines identity as "the beliefs that we use to define our own unique individuality, what makes us unique" (Robbins, 2001). In other words, our identity is who we believe ourselves to be, it isn't who we really might be. To what extent do people's postings on social networking sites like Facebook,

LinkedIn, and Twitter reflect what's really going on for them? Social networking sites, like much else in our civilization, place an insidious pressure on people to behave in certain ways, and to live up to some sort of image. These sites allow people to claim to have unfeasible numbers of friends, links, or followers; contacts who they've never actually met for real. They also enable people to put the most flattering photos on their profiles, giving them an image online. I had one incident recently where I asked someone to give me an introduction to a person they were linked to online, so that I could make direct contact with them. My friend rather embarrassingly had to confess that she didn't know the person, and couldn't remember who he was!

So, with all of these pressures to behave differently with different people in different situations, how healthy is it to be like this? How healthy is it for us to put all sorts of images up about ourselves, and then try to live up to them? What would happen if we didn't do this, and behaved the same way with everybody? This is the root of what I call the *challenge of coherence*. If we visualize our life as a great play and we put on different masks for different parts of it, at what point do we simply become incoherent, both to others and certainly to ourselves? I would argue that, nowadays, we put on an act far too often with the consequence that we lose sight of who we really are. Our whole connection with ourselves is under threat like never before. The loss of things we could have relied on in the past, like stability of family and career, is part of the threat. We are becoming more and more fragmented, with great consequences for our own well-being.

Our Journey to Coherence

This book is divided into three parts. In this part, we will examine the epidemic of personal incoherence that currently exists, and its origins. The core origin, of course, is that as individual human beings we need to rub along with other people to get on in life. As soon as we bring other people into the picture, and the collective organizations that we are all part of, we face pressures to adapt. Some pressure is subtle, some is blatant, and some might be pressure we put on ourselves. Whatever the cause, we learn to adapt. Since early civilization, this has been the case. However, the pressures in modern life are greater than ever before, resulting in fragmented and unfulfilling lives. We will explore different approaches that people have taken in an attempt to discover who they really are. These attempts center on finding a personal identity and an answer to the meaning of life.

In part 2, once you've assessed how coherent you are, I introduce a model that will enable you to enhance your personal coherence, and to retain it more effectively. This model poses four key questions that will enable you to regain control of your life. We also look at how to express your true individuality effectively and authentically. Becoming more fluent in influencing other people is a major contributor to retaining your own shape, particularly when under pressure. As a result, you will feel like you're living your own life.

In part 3, I set out examples of coherent and incoherent responses in a variety of situations, which you may find familiar. We become incoherent as a result of allowing situations and circumstances to manage us. We need to manage them, so concrete examples of what a coherent response looks like in particular situations will be useful. We will contrast these responses with others that involve the wearing of masks.

Let us begin the journey. As you read on, remember the life lessons, and think about the life you'd like to look back on. Oh, and do also retain a sense of humor along the way. By the end, I hope life will look a whole lot better as a result.

We'll begin with a visit to the dark side. Understanding the pressures that we increasingly face is important if we are to do anything about them. The road to personal coherence begins here.

CHAPTER 2

Fragmentation and Masks

We forfeit three-fourths of ourselves in order to be like other people
—Arthur Schopenhauer

Let's start by defining what precisely is meant by the term *fragmentation*. Fragmentation occurs where we are required or require ourselves to behave differently in different situations. In so doing, we are modifying how we would ideally choose to behave, to fit in with the expectations of someone else. Using the theater stage analogy, it means we are putting different masks on for different scenes of the play, and not being our natural self very often. Behaving in a fragmented, noncoherent way has a couple of immediate implications for how we live our lives—and that's before we consider the long-term implications.

First Implication: Loss of Energy

Behaving in a fragmented way costs us energy, a lot of energy. Simply put, it takes energy to behave differently in different situations. The more faces or masks we have to put on, the more energy we spend putting on the show for others.

It takes energy to be different from whom you really are. The more you have to maintain the illusion of difference, the more drained you will end up. Let's be honest now, how many people do you know who reach the end of the day absolutely exhausted? Come to think about it, how many people do you know who wake up totally exhausted? Putting on so many masks comes at a great price to us. We pay that price in terms of our own personal energy, and in extreme circumstances, with our health.

The more acts we have to put on for others, the more stories we have to remember, which takes up mental energy. That is how being fragmented works. By contrast, if you behave as yourself, you don't have to spend as much energy.

However, there is more by way of price to pay, if we lose our own coherence and become fragmented in our personal identity.

Second Implication: Lack of Presence

Another consequence of living a lie is we lose presence. In other words, we don't live for the present moment any more.

Why is this? Again, the answer is simple enough. If our life becomes a succession of acts we put on, we'll always be thinking about our next act, of what we should do when we get to it. We'll either be worrying about the future, or wondering how the current act is going. Is it convincing? Has anyone noticed that I'm acting? If they see something that doesn't quite fit, will I be accepted? Whatever we're thinking about, it isn't what's going on right this moment in front of our eyes.

This is ironic, as the present moment is the only thing we can change. We can't change the past because it has already happened. We can't change the future either, because it has yet to arrive. That leaves us with the present, and we're not even there! We are somewhere else instead, working on the next scene of our life play. We are in the same position as that actor or actress who has to act out the current scene while thinking about what their next line is. That is a great skill, and not one we all possess in the same abundance. Furthermore, acting people do get time out between scenes to recompose themselves. Life does not stop for the rest of us to do this.

The undisputed King of Presence in the modern era is Eckhart Tolle [1]. He wrote a bestselling book called *The power of now*, highlighting the importance of presence in our lives. He also points out how hard it is to be present, and how few of us actually achieve it very often. Tolle talked about the irony of the fact that 90 percent of the population would see themselves as *normal,* whereas in his opinion, normal is *insane.* It is insane to live life in another time zone from the one we are in currently.

I would put it a slightly different way. A fragmented identity makes it impossible to be present, and a key part of presence is to be connected with how we feel in the moment. So we subordinate how we feel in favor of a more rational approach based around the best way to *get by*. In other words, how can I adapt myself?

My Example of Fragmented Personality: Moving to Scotland

When I was 9 years old, my family moved house. We moved from the south east of England to the west of Scotland. In terms of its impact on me, we might as well have moved to a different planet.

I learned pretty rapidly that my English accent was not a welcome one in Scotland, and it marked me out for attention. Attention in those days meant only one thing—trouble.

How did I respond to this situation? I did the obvious thing, and changed my accent to a more Scottish one, and I honed it to perfection to the point that those who didn't know would have assumed I was a local after a couple of years at school. However, when I went home at night, I reverted to an English accent when speaking to my parents. This meant I now had two accents.

My double accented life presented me with one problem, which arose whenever my friends visited the house. Which accent would I use? Either way, there was an expectation on someone's part that I would use their accent. The result for me was stress. I tried to avoid situations where friends and family came into contact, and as a result I was less open with both sets of people.

Another Example of a Fragmented Personality

Another example is Jackie, a woman in her early forties. She eventually succumbed to a depressive illness. Her life had turned into one drudge after another. She was outwardly successful, with a good job, large salary, and a big house which she had renovated herself. She was also in a relationship, and enjoyed good holidays. Her family lived nearby, and showed up regularly. Appearances of course can be deceptive.

In reality, the organization she worked for had a negative, blaming culture that she didn't like. She didn't like the house; it did not feel like hers, despite the fact it was hers. Her relationship was problematic, with her partner regularly pulling her mood down. He was out of work, and showed little inclination to get a job. But he wasn't slow in blaming Jackie for lack of money, or if she did anything wrong. Her family were nosey and judgmental, particularly her parents. They encouraged her to value her outward success, and couldn't understand why she didn't seem happy. No surprise then that Jackie's holidays became the most important thing, as the way to escape from all of this.

At the core of Jackie's fragmentation was the desire to be liked by, and seek approval from, other people. She also had to deal with a family emphasis on *keeping the show on the road*. Her life was not her own because she was living to impress other people, without spending enough time looking at what she wanted.

To use her words, "I just feel tired all the time." It's no wonder she felt like that, given all the energy she was using to put all her masks on.

*

The above examples are contrasting instances of personal fragmentation. One of them was a single issue, and the other affected the person's entire life. In some ways, that is the point. Sometimes the situation will be traumatic, but at other times it won't be. The situations may have started from childhood, but at other times they will have evolved in adulthood. However it happened, when we artificially compartmentalize our life, the result is stress as we try to keep the act going over time.

How many people have you met who behave differently when at work from the way they behave at home? It's no wonder so many people want to avoid the office Christmas party, particularly if they have to bring their partner to the event!

When we are playing all these different roles, a question arises: Which one of these people is the real me?

Our Masks

Let's work a bit more with the idea of masks: What are they exactly? We put all these different masks on for different parts of our life. They contain roles and expectations, and ways to behave acceptably. So, for example, it may be that at work we never contradict the boss, we cannot raise our voice, or even something as simple as we must always wear suitable work attire. Masks are certainly a key aspect of working life for most people, corporate language makes that clear. Why, often when people are fired from or leave their jobs, we hear others say about them *oh well, their face didn't fit.*

Let's consider whether we need to wear a mask, and why that is. Underpinning the mask approach is one assumption. That assumption is: It is *not* OK to be *me.*

After all, if it was OK to be me, I wouldn't need to wear a mask. As a result of this, we put ourselves in disguise. That is OK to some extent, as long as we realize that's what we're doing. But the risk of masks is that we lose ourselves in wearing them.

The most dramatic examples of this, and the consequences that go with them, are to be found in those who spend much of their life on the stage. Actors and actresses, rock and pop stars, TV personalities and sports stars all routinely spend their lives on the stage. The results can be seen all around us. A few high-profile casualties included Elvis Presley, Michael Jackson, Amy Winehouse, and Michael Hutchence. In many cases, these people were clearly lacking self-esteem and put on a face for the benefit of others, while feeling empty and sad inside. These are the ultimate casualties.

Behind them though is an army of people in these professions with drink and drug problems, on therapy, with diet issues, or suffering from depression. Apparent success does not alleviate this issue either, with the likes of ex-England rugby star Jonny Wilkinson openly admitting to suffering serious depression while at the height of his career, which included being a world champion.

Success does not feel like success when it comes with this price tag attached. Before we move on, let's consider where these masks originate from. There are a number of places, many of them found in childhood.

Mask 1: Convention

Society has evolved with conventional ways of doing many things. These include the religion we are brought up with, acceptable ways to learn at school, fashions in our teenage years, and *custom and practice*. We are brought up on conventions across the board, and there is usually a price to be paid for not following them. At one extreme we can face disciplinary action or even expulsion for failure to comply with the accepted rules and customs. But an equally damaging penalty is the risk of criticism, ostracism, or being seen as a maverick, which doesn't do much for our position.

Nationalism and national characteristics, our age, and where we work all carry expectations for how we will behave. Most of us, to a greater or lesser extent, will choose to behave in accordance with those rules.

Mask 2: The Way We Do Things

Some rules are softer in that they are not made explicit to us. But we learn over time how to behave, perhaps when we've been burned for breaking the rules. The cultures of organizations we work in are one example of this.

I remember hearing a brilliant example of how things evolve without thinking, and what the result can look like. The story centers on a zoo, and a cage full of monkeys. As you read it, enjoy the story, and the irony. It is based on work carried out with rhesus monkeys [2].

The Zoo Story

Six monkeys lived in a zoo cage, with plenty of space for them to play. In the center of the cage stood a ladder, which led up to a large hook for bananas to be lowered into the cage. The monkeys happily ate bananas by climbing the ladder so they could reach the banana hook.

One day, without warning, the zookeeper instituted an experiment. He lowered the bananas onto the hook, and the hungry monkeys fell over each other to climb the ladder and get their feast. As soon as the first monkey got to the top, the zookeeper turned a hosepipe on, and gave all six monkeys a thorough drenching.

On day 2, the same thing happened. When the first monkey got to the top of the ladder, the zookeeper soaked all six monkeys with the hosepipe.

By day 3, things changed a little. The monkeys looked at the bananas on the hook, but the rush to the top had ceased. Then one monkey decided to go for it. As soon as he reached the ladder, he was attacked by the other five monkeys, who by now were fed up with the soakings they had received. The victim was given a pasting by the others.

By day 4, the zookeeper had substituted a new monkey for one of the old ones. So, when the bananas arrived, the new monkey made a beeline for the ladder, and was promptly set upon by the other five. He was given a good beating, with the monkey who'd been beaten up the day before being especially vigilant in dishing out the punishment!

On each of days 5, 6, 7, 8, and 9, the other five original monkeys were replaced by new monkeys, one a day. On each day, the new arrival went for the ladder, and was set upon by the other five.

By day 10, all six monkeys knew not to go up the ladder to eat the bananas for risk of being attacked. None of them knew the original reason why going up the ladder was bad. They had never seen the hosepipe or witnessed the soakings. None of them understand why it was necessary to attack rebel monkeys who approach the ladder. All of them now make out as if they aren't hungry, and don't see the bananas.

And that, my readers, is how organizational cultures evolve!

To those of you who work in organizations, just how true is that? Too true, in many instances.

Mask 3: Expectation and Approval

There is nothing like other people's expectations to make us put a mask on. Expectations can come from us, or from other people, and the result is much the same. What we believe to be true will govern how we behave; both our beliefs about ourselves and about how we think other people see us.

Beliefs we hold and intentions we state that contain the words *ought* or *should* are particularly to be watched. *Ought* and *should* are words that are about what other people expect from us, or what we expect from ourselves, rather than being things we really want to do. The more times we use words like these, the less coherent we are likely to be, and the greater the number of masks we have to wear just to get by.

Most of us have a need for approval, both from ourselves and from others. The greater that need, the more we will put a mask on that we think gets us that approval.

In my many meetings with people considering making a change to their career or life, the conversations almost always come down to a conflict between what the heart wants and what the head says can be done. What the head tells us usually comes down to a combination of conditioning, upbringing, and expectations of other people around us of what we must deliver. If ever there was a case of putting masks on, this is it.

Our Wardrobe of Masks

Given the above, we have a wardrobe of masks that we put on depending on the situation. Each mask has been designed to be used in particular situations (and in the case of work we literally have a wardrobe of masks, called suits). Wearing these masks, we adapt ourselves to each environment we're in. Another way of looking at this is we bend the *real me* out of shape in an attempt to fit in, to get approval. We put all these fronts on for different situations, hiding the *real me*. This plethora of masks, behaviors, approaches, and styles means that other people don't see who we really are. It is often said that we create our own reality. In adopting our masks, we literally do this.

The Problem with Masks

There are many potential issues with masks. One simply is that other people don't see the *real you*, and you don't see the *real other* either. This makes it rather difficult to build any kind of meaningful relationship. Taken to its extreme, I'm sure we've all encountered at least one marriage where it's obvious that the whole show is just a big act put on for the benefit of others. When all the guests have gone, the two partners will have little to talk about, if indeed they're talking at all. It all exists on a superficial level. When we wear a mask all the time, it is hard to end up with any relationship that is better than superficial.

However, I want to focus on a deeper problem with masks, which arises when we carry so many of them. The risk is that we forget who we really are, and lose our own sense of meaningful personal identity. Then we are in big trouble. We literally get weighed down by the number of masks we carry in life. What's more, we may not even be aware of some of the masks we wear.

Masks can, however, become very visible when circumstances change. For an example of this, take an outwardly successful executive. Jim was an Information Technology (IT) executive, who had built up his own business. His venture was so successful that it expanded rapidly, and other directors were brought into the company. Jim, at the height of his powers, was feted by national IT publications as a great example of entrepreneurial activity and vision.

It didn't last. Eventually, there was a board level disagreement during a turbulent time for the industry, and Jim ended up on the wrong side of the disagreement. He was fired from the job, leaving him with the need to find a new one. When I first met Jim, he was a shadow of the formerly successful, confident executive staring out from those outdated IT publications. His self-confidence had evaporated, and he was fundamentally incapable of holding a conversation with another human being. When asked to list how many friends he had, he didn't think that he had many, and nor did he feel he could ever ask a favor of any of his friends. What a sad place to be in. Basically, his job was a huge mask that enabled Jim to project a personality onto the stage of IT. But once the job was removed, there was nothing left behind.

Now you might say that you do actually wear different masks, but that you need them to survive. Of course, there is a need to adapt our behavior at times to different situations. The questions are why we are adapting, and to what extent we do so. To use an analogy, the Statue of Liberty may look different from different angles, but it is always recognizably the Statue of Liberty. It is recognizable whether you see it from 50 yards away or 50 miles. But to what extent are you always you when looked at from different angles?

Let's put this to the test with an exercise.

Exercise: Who Am I?

To what extent then are you being yourself? How do different people describe you? Take the following checklist of questions and ask four or five people to answer them, thinking about you. Ask them to write down their answers, and give the answers back to you.

Ideally, you want to ask a cross section of people to answer these questions, perhaps including family members, friends, work colleagues, or even your boss. Include people who know you well, and one or two who may only know you a little.

The questions they should answer are:

1. What do you think my ambitions in life are?
2. What sorts of things do I like, and dislike?
3. What would you say are my most important values, or principles, by which I live?
4. What is the most important thing in my life?
5. If you were describing my personality to someone else, what three words would you use?

Once you have all your responses, compare and contrast the results, and work through the following questions yourself.

- Do you recognize yourself from what they are saying?
- To what extent are they describing the person you'd like to be?
- How similar or different are their views of you?
- How coherent or fragmented are you?

＊

I believe that the masks we adopt are a response essentially to three questions we learn to ask ourselves. They parallel the questions we ask ourselves in a fashion clothes shop when we're looking for a different outfit (not something I do all that often, but those of you who regularly engage in retail therapy might recognize these questions!). Go on then, try that new outfit on.

- How do I look?
- What will other people think?
- How do I gain success, or avoid failure?

The third question is about whether we want to stand out (e.g., at a wedding) or not stand out (e.g., at a funeral). When we elect to put masks on later in life, we are essentially dressing ourselves up, and so we ask ourselves these same questions.

Of course, some people will also ask a fourth question when buying themselves an outfit.

• Do I like what I see?

In essence, this is the question I'm asking you to bear in mind as you investigate just what your own wardrobe of masks look like. But I also want you to remember that, even if you like the masks, having lots of them effectively bends the real you out of shape, and this rarely results in a happy life. So how do you start to let go of the masks that envelop your life and prevent you from really living?

Before we can answer this question, we need first to understand more about how we acquired the wardrobe we are lumbered with at present.

So, let's look in more depth at why it is that we fragment in the first place, and adopt all these masks. Understanding the sources of fragmentation will help us to spot all the masks we do actually have, because not all of our masks will be visible to us right now.

CHAPTER 3

Three Sources
of Fragmentation

To be yourself in a world that is constantly trying to make you something else is the greatest accomplishment

—Ralph Waldo Emerson

In this chapter, we're going to look at the three main sources of fragmentation—our childhood, our society, and the workplace. Each of these areas has a significant impact on our behavior, resulting in our acquisition of the masks we go on to wear for the rest of our lives. Let us begin at the start, with childhood.

1. Childhood

Virtually every psychologist in the world will tell you that the key aspects of human personality are fully formed by around the age of nine. In our formative years, when we are taught how to behave, we are almost completely dependent on other people for our survival and upbringing. This includes food, shelter, love, and companionship. Starting with our family and then broadening out to school and other authorities in our life, we learn how to behave.

Many of the lessons we learn early in life are not ones our parents might have intended. They are the things that we remember though, and their impact on us leads us to modify our behavior—for good, ill, or maybe even both. Other people influence our early behavior too; extended family, siblings, even childhood friends, and encounters during our early schooldays. We are influenced by what goes on around us, particularly when we're in contact with more powerful people.

I'm sure you will be able to see lessons from your own childhood as you look back. They will all be different, and they will all have impacted on the extent to which you allow your real self to come out in life.

Stages of Childhood

There are four key stages in childhood, and each of these stages marks a shift in the nature of what we learn. Let's look at each of them in turn. Please note that the years in brackets for each stage are an indication of when that stage comes into play. The exact time for each transition will vary between children. However, these age ranges do fit my own childhood experience, and those of many other people I have met. As you read, let's see what you remember.

Stage 1: Unconscious and Subconscious Evolution (First 2 Years of Life)

Most of us won't have any memories of events during this stage in our lives. My first memory isn't until about 2½ years old. During this stage, we are utterly dependent on the key figures in our life, and for most (but not all) of us, that will be one or two parents, and possibly a few other family members. These people affect our development as human beings, but our learning is at a largely unconscious or subconscious level. To uncover this stuff means therapy or regression type treatments, and that is beyond the subject matter of this book.

Stage 2: Learning about Myself (2 to 5 Years)

Somewhere around 2 years old, we start to become more aware of *me*. We realize that we have our own unique identity, and with that we have our own needs that we want to have met. By this stage, we have also acquired the language skills to start expressing our needs.

This period can become a power struggle between us and the authority figures who know better, as we try to get what we want. Many parents see this period as the *terrible two's*, as it is at this stage where children learn to assert themselves more. We also start to discover what sorts of behaviors are seen as good and bad. We then have a choice on whether to comply or to rebel. Depending on the options we choose here, we put on masks for the first time, even if they are infant masks.

We remember more of what goes on day to day, and more of these memories stick with us for the rest of our lives, especially events that were emotionally significant. Things like births, bereavements, or first days at school.

Stage 3: Learning about Relationships (from 5 to 10 Years)

During this phase, we start to learn more about relationships. We have already realized our own uniqueness in stage 2, but here we learn that we are part of a wider community of children (and adults). We realize that we are all different, if only because we live in different bodies. We relate more to others, and it is during this period that many of us make our first real friends. Childhood friends who become lifetime friends are commonplace at this stage.

We get on with some people, and not with others. We learn to like and dislike. We also start to realize how we compare to others, partly through our own experience, and partly through what we're told by others. We remember things like *he's good musically*, *she's shy*, and we learn things like *I'm not as strong as he is*, or *I'm shorter than she is*. These messages eventually coalesce into a belief system that governs significant elements of our behavior from this point on. This system of learning moves on to one final stage, which develops as we begin to build relationships.

Stage 4: Learning about Our Fit (from 10 to 16 Years)

In stage 4, we start to hit the teenage years with everything that goes with that, including being interested in girls or boys. The increased need to make ourselves appealing to people we're attracted to drives all sorts of behavior change. We dress differently, talk differently, and model ourselves on people we see as successful. This alone causes us to collect masks like there's no tomorrow. However, the awakening of our sexuality is only one development during this stage.

We also learn about our fit into wider society. Fads and fashions become more important, and we seek the approval of other people more than we did before. Fashions are particularly important during our teenage years. To put it another way, if you don't follow the fashion, you don't fit in, and for most people fitting in matters. Consequently, we learn to suspend our judgment on what we like, and what's good for us, and allow others to influence us on this. Hence the pressures to try drugs, drinking, and smoking, all things that deep down we know aren't good for us. Pressures to diet, dress a particular way, follow particular fashion, sport and music icons, become difficult to resist.

By stage 4, we have learned to keep a wardrobe of masks, and to use them regularly to get the approval of others—and possibly of ourselves.

Approval and Disapproval

In an ideal world, we want to get the approval of other people as we grow up. However, arguably more important than this is the need to avoid disapproval. It was Dr. Eric Berne [1] who highlighted the role of positive and negative strokes to an individual's well-being. A positive stroke was positive recognition, for example receiving praise for something done well. A negative stroke, by contrast, was disapproval or criticism for poor behavior or performance.

Dr. Berne's conclusion was that the best outcome for a young child is to receive positive strokes. However, it is better for a child to receive negative strokes than to receive none. No recognition at all is the nightmare scenario for a child. This explains why often children will misbehave as a way to get their parents' attention.

For many of us, the idea of seeking disapproval will seem like a strange one. However, children will be highly motivated to avoid the disapproval of people who matter to them. Hence, we should not lose sight of the impact of disapproval on the strategies we have learned to get by, as we mature.

Your formative years will have had a major impact on the range of masks you wear in life. Childhood sets the scene for the stage play to come. But there's more than one playwright in this play, and the other two are becoming stronger as we move through the second decade of the 21st century. The society we live in is one of them, along with the pressures that go with it.

2. Societal Pressures

In this section, I plan to focus on five areas where society exerts considerable pressure on us as individuals to start building our own masks, and put them on. These areas are:

- The way we are educated
- The impact of fashions and advertising
- The effects of globalization
- The role of the media in shaping our views and expectations, and
- The cult of expertise we are increasingly faced with.

Let's examine each of them in turn.

Societal Pressures: Education

Most adults will readily admit that their education had a fundamental impact on their subsequent life, for good or otherwise. Cast your mind back for a moment to the time when you had to make decisions about the subjects you studied at school or college. What advice did you receive about what to do? Was it, do the subjects you're good at, and enjoy? Or was it, do subjects that will get you a job? I bet for most of you, the advice and pressure was on you to do the latter.

In this way, we are pushed into things that will get us a job or career. Academic subjects like maths, the sciences, and languages get the nod during this debate about our future. These are subjects that primarily engage our left brain, the side of our head that deals with the rational, thinking stuff. Alternatively, if we're not seen as academic, we may be pushed down the practical route, with subjects that might get us into employment.

Either way, we're not generally encouraged to use our creative talents at the business end of our schooldays. Art and music, for example, are often viewed as fringe options. Education does not encourage us in the use of our right brain, the creative, intuitive part of us.

Much has changed in education over the last 50 years, but it's arguable whether the basics have changed much. Society's assumption is that the purpose of education is to get us employment. Anything wider than that is largely given lip service. What's more, the emphasis nowadays on benchmarks for schools, and on more and more exams for children, has placed the emphasis of education on passing exams rather than learning. The trouble is that passing exams and learning are not the same thing.

A few years ago, I watched a brilliant lecture by Sir Ken Robinson [2], given in 2006 to a Technology, Entertainment and Design (TED) conference. His lecture graphically outlines the consequences arising from the evolution of the education systems in the Western world. He quotes Pablo Picasso, who said that "all children are born artists. The problem is to remain an artist as we grow up" (Robinson, 2006).

Robinson's conclusion was that the primary purpose of the education system is to produce university professors—because that is what the education system itself rewards. To use his own words, "many highly talented, brilliant, creative thinkers believe they're not," as a result of being educated in the Western world (Robinson, 2006).

Some highly talented, creative thinkers march on regardless. Albert Einstein was famously rejected by his Munich schoolmaster with the words "you will never amount to very much." For a more recent example, go to Professor Sir John Gurdon, who won the Nobel Prize in 2012 for his role in stem cell research, along with Shinya Yamanaka. Sir John subsequently revealed his school report, age 15, in which he was ranked 250th out of 250 in Biology at Eton [3].

The actual wording of his school report read as follows:

It has been a disastrous half. His work has been far from satisfactory. His prepared stuff has been badly learnt, and several of his test pieces have been torn over; one of such pieces of prepared work scored 2 marks out of a possible 50. His other work has been equally bad, and several times he has been in trouble, because he will not listen, and will insist on doing his work in his own way. I believe he has ideas about becoming a scientist; on his present showing this is quite ridiculous, if he can't learn simple Biological facts he would have no chance of doing the work of a specialist, and it would be sheer waste of time, both on his part, and of those who have to teach him. (Nobelprize.org, 2012)

In other words, the boy was a nonconformist, refusing to mask himself up and play the game. Good thing too, considering the results. But how many other potentially brilliant people would have succumbed to this game, masked up, and forfeited what they might have achieved, and been?

Consider what happens when the media spotlight falls on the education system. A few years back, in the United Kingdom, there was a furore about meaningless college courses. Film and media studies was one of the castigated subjects. The claim was that film and media studies didn't teach you anything meaningful that would get you a job. This illustrates the point that society's primary expectation of education in the Western world is that it helps people find a livelihood. Education is not geared to helping people engage with their own unique individuality and creativity. That's why schools are assessed by using league tables of throughput, and numbers of exam passes. Schools are increasingly treated as factories.

This factory emphasis and the study to get a job mentality are ironic, given what's happening at the moment. In 2012, there was evidence that companies recruiting graduates were increasingly ignoring graduates who didn't have a first-class degree. With many graduates applying for every job, employers can afford to be fussy in preselecting graduates to interview. Meanwhile, the need to take loans out to fund studies is leading universities to shorten the length of their courses to attract students. In 2010, the BPP University College in London announced the launch of a new 2-year law degree, which duly attracted 50 percent more applicants than expected.

The school as factory model should come as no surprise. The next step most of us take once we leave school or university is to try to find a job—and go into a real factory, or the nearest thing we have to a factory nowadays. We will return to the work pressures we face shortly. But for now, let's consider another aspect of society that puts pressure on us to modify our behavior by putting on masks.

Societal Pressures: Fashions and Advertising

Do you remember your teenage years? For many of us, these years were an exciting time of discovery, exploration, and trying out different things.

But, whatever those years were like for you, one other factor was in play. If we are aware in early childhood of our own unique individuality, we become much more aware in late childhood and teenage years of the power of the collective. We start noticing other people our age, and what they do. Most of us have some desire to conform, to fit in with someone or some group. There is a subtle pressure not to stand out. Teenagers who do stand out are likely to suffer for it; bullying, ridicule, ostracism, or being ignored. Do you remember those children who stood out at school? How were they treated? Of course, a handful may not have minded standing out. Perhaps they were strong characters. However, most would choose to conform, and stand out less.

In our teens, the desire to belong expresses itself in fashions. Fashions like having the latest games, or wearing similar clothes as our friends become *must do* things. In the 1950s, we had the specter of mods and rockers fighting in towns and cities up and down the United Kingdom. With their customs, styles of dress and talk, and musical tastes, you could choose to be the one or the other. But you couldn't, ever, like both!

Not much has changed since then, even if there are a lot more musical options to choose from. The pressure to conform remains the same. I see the ads on TV, in cinemas, and in magazines, not to mention online, telling us how to conform. What to wear, how to talk, which TV programs to like, what music to buy, what makeup to wear, I could go on and on— the advertising certainly does. I've heard many parents comment how children are expected to grow up a lot earlier than previous generations did. Twelve-year olds in this generation look like what 16-year-olds did a generation or two ago, dressing in an adult way before they have an adult brain.

The play continues afterward. How much of what we buy and do is conditioned by the fads and fashions that go on around us? What car to have, what holiday to take, what clothes to wear, and even what mobile phone to have, are all conditioned by advertising and fashions.

Societal Pressures: Globalization

With the development of TV and the Internet, we have never had so much opportunity to watch whatever we want. We can also make contact with people all over the world. Some of these developments have been a force for good. One obvious example, in 2011, were the pro-democracy demonstrations in Iran that were so ruthlessly put down. Demonstrators with video cameras recorded what was going on, and posted the images online. These were picked up in turn by the media, so ensuring that the Iranian Government's behavior was highlighted to the world.

In addition, the role of Facebook in the Arab Spring in 2011 highlighted how easy it was for a movement to gain rapid credibility even when faced by authoritarian regimes. Across the Arab world, the regular pictures of demonstrating people and casualties focused world opinion on the events that were going on, with regimes toppling as a result.

So, this is a good thing, right?

There is always another side to the story. How about the peer pressure generated by the TV and Internet? One example of this was the summer of discontent in the United Kingdom in 2011, when cities throughout the country were engulfed in flames, with rioters, looters, and muggers out in force. Clearly, social networking sites had a different impact in this case, proving a less positive influence. There is no doubt that people with a criminal intent took advantage of this situation. However, what about the other people who were there? Did they go out to see what was going on, because everyone else was doing the same? If so, they would easily be caught up in the events during those hot nights. The chance to appear on TV and online will have contributed to the numbers who went out, and ended up on the rampage. While the globalization of the media and of news didn't cause what happened, it may have contributed to the scale of what happened.

The role of the media in forging society, or the breakdown of society, was highlighted to me dramatically while on holiday a few years ago, in Peru. On this particular day, I took a trip to Lake Titicaca, the highest navigable lake in the world. It is a truly breathtakingly beautiful lake. This boat trip took me to some idyllic islands, which were entirely man made from reeds. Incredibly, the staple diet of the islanders included reeds, all the houses were made from reeds, and all their furniture was reed made too. One woman proudly showed me round her house, and the only thing that wasn't built from reeds was the satellite TV in the corner, next to her bed.

We were welcomed to the island by women and children dancing and singing, a thoroughly charming, entrancing reception. I can hardly envisage anyone being welcomed where I live in this way! Everyone was smiling, and as a trained observer of body language that has taught me to tell the difference between genuine and false smiles, these ones looked genuine. Everyone looked healthy too, none of the obesity so prevalent in the Western world.

So, what was wrong with this picture?

The last word of that question is the clue: picture. That TV in the woman's living-cum-bedroom is what was wrong. The one thing missing from the village were most of the teenagers and people in their early twenties. TV had given them a view of the outside world, and they had left in pursuit of it. In other words, the children are leaving this island, and it will likely be a dead community within a generation or two.

To me, that looks like a case of paradise lost. Will those lost generations be happier than their predecessors on that island? I don't think so. What this story does highlight though is the power of TV, and the images conveyed through it. If only those images were real. The nearest city to this island did not look like the sort of place you'd want anyone you knew to live in, unless you didn't like them!

Of course, that image of how others live is not necessarily an accurate one. It doesn't only happen through TV either; just look at the Internet. We now have the opportunity to become our own media manipulators, to manage how we are seen by others. Take a look at the explosion of Facebook accounts with people posting everything from updates on their lives, to photos, building personal profiles, and talking to people they didn't even know existed before the advent of social networking sites.

Again, some of this is good. It gives us the opportunity to swap ideas, get to know people with similar interests, and keep in touch with friends. But consider this question: to what extent does the image of someone's life put online reflect their real life? Is it just another mask we put up for other people? It may look to others like I have a life, but do I really have one? We give ourselves an image to live up to, and we try to live up to it.

Societal Pressures: The Media

We've already touched on the role of TV and the Internet. However, an additional dimension is presented by the role of the media, in the form of TV news, current affairs services, and newspapers.

Have you ever noticed how the media engenders fear in most of us? It has long been a truism that the media latch onto bad news as manna from heaven, and many of us comply in this game. War spirit, and pulling together in crises, are legendary things. Even in my childhood, I remember *News at Ten*, when the last story was always a lighthearted or good news story, to make us all feel better. It was usually the only good news story out there, and more often than not it involved an animal or a child. All else was crisis, war, murder, and crime.

To illustrate this point, here is a selection of news stories, from a few media sources as of March 30, 2015.

BBC Website

> Pension data 'sales' investigated
> Parents rarely spot child obesity
> Iran nuclear talks near key deadline
> PM warns voters of stark choice
> Fraud office fined £180k for breach
> False allegations 'blight' teaching
> DNA of 78 Germanwings victims found

Daily Mail Website

> Your pension secrets sold to conmen for five pence
> We know everything about you: Sinister boast of data boss
> One fifth of girls under eleven have already been on a diet
> Now jihadi bride school is centre of terror probe
> More than a fifth of school staff falsely accused by pupils of abuse or bullying
> Prepare for landing? Hopefully . . . we'll see: Chilling words of crash co-pilot
> Expert warns Labour plans would leave £30billion black hole in economy

Fox News Website

Netanyahu accuses Iran of trying to 'conquer the entire Middle East'

Tsunami warning issued for parts of Pacific after earthquake

Prosecutors expected to rest their case in Boston Marathon bombing trial

Florida City ponders spring break restrictions after 7 shot at house party

2 bodies found at NYC building explosion site

Arab summit: Yemen airstrikes to go on until rebels withdraw

Germanwings black box transcript reveals captain pleading with co-pilot

*

Clearly, these news headlines are more likely to engender fear in us, than to encourage hope. I'm not saying that this is the intention of the media, but it is definitely the impact.

This is all very well, but hasn't the media focus on bad news always been the case? The answer, of course, is yes. What made the largest headlines in 1901, if it wasn't the death of Queen Victoria? In 1912, it was the sinking of the Titanic. In 1963, it must have been the assassination of John F Kennedy. Stories engendering fear have always been the dominant theme.

What has changed, however, is the media's access to events on this planet. It's hard to envisage anything happening on Earth now that doesn't get recorded. But the biggest change is that news is now a 24-hour day event. Visit a workplace, bank, or any public place nowadays, and the latest news is all around us. All the time.

This onslaught of news stories engenders fear and more fear. Fear of war, economic catastrophe, losing pensions, becoming ill with the latest epidemic—and that's just a few fears. When we become more fearful, we tend to shut down. Hopes of a better life and achieving our dreams become submerged in the need to stay secure and survive. Instead of hoping for better, we are simply grateful to retain what we have. Mediocrity becomes acceptable because it is better than despair.

Curiously, the impact of daily news is reinforced by the rest of what we see on TV. Consider the myriad of soap operas we have on our screens. Thirty years ago, the stories were relatively believable and normal, but that has changed in favor of dramatic events like murders, rapes, terrorism, and violence. In the name of entertainment, the word *fear* becomes more dominant.

With dramatics for entertainment and mediocrity in our daily lives, what better way to round off the day than by watching the hopes of people wanting to make it big go up in smoke? Yes, it's time for Reality TV to put in an appearance. From *Big Brother* to *Pop Idol* to the range of cooking, singing, and dancing competitions, it's the opportunity to see people either make it, or to chuckle at their failures. What's more, we can even vote on who we want! A case of reality TV becoming more reality than real life is. More people now vote on TV than do in elections. But we need to see someone succeeding to believe that success is possible, because it isn't possible in our world. In our world, as Marianne Williamson [4] once said, we fear our own power, along with fearing everything else.

This fear is reinforced by politicians who frankly love a good crisis. I mean, how many wars have we had? Wars on terror, holy wars, hygiene wars in hospitals, wars on cancer. These crises have one other effect— they lead us to suspend judgment and accept things that we wouldn't otherwise.

As an example of this, look no further than those terrible terrorist attacks in the United States on September 11, 2001. We can all remember where we were when we first saw those horrific news images. But look what we accepted as a result of that day. Two wars in Afghanistan and Iraq, the first unwinnable, and the second irrelevant to the cause of fighting terrorism. The vast majority of the U.S. and UK public chose to support their political leaders at the time of both declarations of war. The message could not be clearer: crisis results in compliance from most people. That's why politicians emphasize crises and the media act as the prime crisis cheerleader in our society. No wonder most people draw their horns in, and give up. So, airline passengers now routinely undergo stop searches that would have been utterly unacceptable 20 years ago.

In the end, many of us spend most of our lives failing in one way or another. Not because we are failures, but because for one reason or another, we chose not to try to succeed. The role of the media in establishing that failure climate should not be underestimated. Nor, as we will see later, do we have to accept this fate.

Societal Pressures: The Role of Expertise

When we are young, we might pick up the message that we don't know very much, and be encouraged to defer to people who know more than we do. During this period, we are often expected to defer to parents, relatives, teachers, and other authority figures.

What can happen in adulthood is that we simply change who it is we defer to—and in modern society, there are no shortages of experts to defer to. Modern society suffers from an epidemic of expertise. All you have to do is to switch on your TV. You will find experts on everything from diet to psychological illness, financial advice, IT, economics, household budgeting, baby health, alcohol, and law. Had he been alive today, Winston Churchill might have said that "never in the cause of human history have there been so many experts that we owe so much to." There is no area of modern life that experts don't pass their judgment and advice on, and often the experts don't even agree with each other.

I am not saying that we should not have experts in life. I am saying that we should not simply defer to them. When we do, expertise simply becomes another mask, a mask we may adopt ourselves on things we are *expert* on. But it also leads us to put a mask on when faced with expertise, if we're not careful. This mask is one of deference and suspension of our own judgment.

Societal Pressures: The Question

As we have seen, formal and informal institutions in society are very powerful. From our political leaders and the media to the subtler advertising and social networking, society exercises a huge impact on us. In most cases, these institutions create a need to conform and fit in. We do just this, playing our roles as good citizen (or subject), aspiring purchaser, fashion follower, and social image maker.

But, in the middle of all this, where has our own life gone?

3. Work

Most of us spend on average about half our waking life in the office or at work. What happens at work will have a major effect on us, so we're now going to look at some of these effects.

Applying for a Job

You need to work, right? To pay the bills, make a living, and to do those things you always wanted to do, like go on holidays. So, you apply for a job. What happens?

First, consider the job advert you answered. What is it the prospective employer expects you to do? Of course, there will be the technical side to the role, with all the jargon that goes with it. However, then you consider the other qualities the employer appears to be looking for. They often include things like ability to work to tight deadlines under significant pressure, being able to influence everyone in the company at whatever level, being dynamic, high powered, and thriving on a heavy workload.

Words and phrases like hearts and minds, quick thinking, visionary, enterprising, thrusting, and high energy are all commonplace. These are the kinds of words employers use when describing their jobs in advertisements. I have taken a selection of recent quotations from job advertisements in circulation on one particular day. It does not really matter what the jobs themselves are. Just consider the wording.

- Develop tactical guerrilla brand media strategies with our agency partners to deliver the communications strategies.
- The CEO will expect you to be highly organized, diligent, proactive and innovative, with the self-motivation and resilience to deliver an outstanding service.
- If you are confident, tenacious, passive, and approachable, with a degree of assertiveness and have a good sense of humor, then this could be for you.

- You will be a confident, dynamic, self-motivated and driven individual with a flexible approach, with the ability to put forward creative ideas and solutions that add value to the business.
- To be ultimately successful in this role you need to be a consistent high achiever, driven, resilient, and motivated by targets.

*

Another illustration of this whole issue came from a professional friend of mine. She applied for a job on the recommendation of a recruiter, who thought she ticked all the boxes the employer was looking for. However, she was not even offered an interview. The reason the employer gave for rejecting her was that "I do not want to interview her as her CV does not demonstrate that she goes above and beyond."

The question this comment raised in my, and my friend's, mind is *above and beyond* what exactly? To quote the joke, "I don't think I can do this job. Oh, hang on a second, this is my job being advertised!"

Looking at the above advertisements, do you feel any pressure to become someone else? Most of us do feel that pressure. But then this is just the job advertisement. What then happens when you actually start work?

The Working Day: A Personal Example

Let me give you a trivial example of how I discovered what work was like. My first job was with the Postal Service, and to be fair my first manager was a good one. He was the kind of manager who tried to look after people who were new to the organization, and I learned a lot from him.

However, on this particular day, he sat me down to give me a piece of advice. He thought it would help my career prospects if I could learn to walk faster! What was his rationale for this? It was that, if other people saw me rushing, they would assume I was busy. It was a defense against being seen as underemployed. So, I was to look stressed even if I wasn't feeling stressed. As a result of this advice, my behavior fragmented, and I started to walk faster when at work. However, I reverted to my more leisurely pace when I left the office.

Now this is a trivial example, as I've already said. However, the Postal Service demonstrated the same approach in a less trivial case. This was the case of a directive to postal staff that they deliver the mail, while managing an average walking speed of 4 miles per hour (or 6 km per hour). Not surprisingly, this directive was exposed as practically impossible to achieve, and in the end, the business backed down from insisting on this requirement.

Both of the above examples illustrate how we are expected to modify our behavior at work. It has been like that since the dawn of capitalism in the Victorian era. Most people cheerfully carry a work wardrobe. Whether it's the suit for the city or office, or working overalls for a factory, or a uniform for a retail outlet or catering establishment, the majority of the working population run with the idea that we wear one sort of clothing for work. At the end of the working day, we change to go home, or when we arrive home. In other words, the way we dress is a mask at work. We dress to impress, or at least to comply with the expectations of other people where we work, particularly those in authority.

The nature of the clothing mask has evolved over time, and is the most visible manifestation of corporate life. We see it from the handmade suits and shoes of top corporate executives, through to middle management's more standard tailoring, and the starter suits worn by those in their first job. But then, to avoid being completely condemned by the fashion police, and to appear trendy, many organizations now cling to the idea of having dress down Fridays. However, it cannot be a complete free for all, even on dress down days. I've seen Human Resource departments wring their hands at what clothing is and is not acceptable on dress down days. I need not mention the business that allowed the wearing of casual wear, unless made by the fashion house French Connection (or FCUK for short!)

The nature of work has changed significantly during the last 30 years. What's more, the way it has changed has undermined our own personal identities in a more fundamental way by demanding that we install more and more masks. I will illustrate what has changed with a further example.

Working in the 1960s, and Now

A few years ago, I had a really interesting conversation with a woman called Ann about the nature of work. She talked about her experience of work, compared to her father's experience. It made for interesting listening.

What did she say?

She worked in a modern office, in a reasonably successful job. Yet she felt disempowered, and not in control of her work or her life. She spent most of her waking hours at work, a situation many people could identify with. Her working days comprised huge emotional stress, and at the end of the day, it was all she could do to go home and collapse at night (usually in front of the TV). She had little energy for anything else.

As Ann relayed this story, my first thought was, so what's unique about this? This is a story I hear far too often for comfort. Long hours, poor work life balance, not enjoying it, and so on. But what she went on to say was fascinating. She contrasted her work experiences with those of her father, with whom she had a close relationship. He had been a coal miner, and to her mind, he was a much more empowered person than she was at work.

My first reaction—what? You mean those guys who spent all day down a mine, in dangerous conditions, with dictatorial bosses and union militancy, who had no real choice about what job they did, were more empowered than middle managers working in the modern era. Are you kidding? But no, it turns out she had a point. She talked of the banter down the coal mine, of a real camaraderie between work mates. I guess we saw some of that with those brave Chilean miners who were finally rescued in 2010 after more than 2 months of being trapped underground following a mine accident. I remember watching live on TV as those miners were brought out in a space-like capsule that had been sunk into the ground, big enough to bring out one man at a time. Would these miners have survived those dark days alone, not knowing if they would ever be rescued, without a strong sense of comradeship? Personally, I doubt it.

So, Ann's father had comradeship to see him through. At the end of the day, even doing a job that was physically exhausting in a way few jobs are nowadays, he had plenty of energy to participate in community life afterward. This is in sharp contrast to Ann's collapsing in the armchair statement.

Ann's final comment resonated with me strongly, and it is this that I want to explore more with you now. She said the following words: "The thing about my dad was that he was able to be himself."

This was a catalyst for me to explore what has changed in the world of work that makes it harder to be ourselves. I will now take you through a model that I believe will throw light on why work is less fulfilling now than for previous generations.

The Doing Thinking and Being Model

This model is most often applied to developing leadership in work organizations. It shows that, to be an effective leader, you have to get three things right: doing, thinking, and being.

Doing: Leaders need to do stuff, otherwise they aren't leaders. Taking action and leading from the front would form part of this.

Thinking: Leaders need to demonstrate their intellectual capability, to understand what's going on, and think through potentially complex problems. Otherwise, they may be acting to address the wrong issues. This, of course, would not amount to very effective leadership!

Being: It's not just about how we think or what we do, effective leadership is also about how we are. It's important to lead in line with our own personal values and core purpose. We behave authentically and with integrity rather than putting on a false front, which others would see through sooner or later anyway. If thinking is about the head, being is about the heart.

I have spent much of my career developing both current and potential future organizational leaders. What has struck me most about leadership is the gap between rhetoric and reality in most organizations. On the one hand, the rhetoric is generally about developing leadership throughout organizations, not just at the very top. After all, with the pace of change, speed of technological development, and volatility of markets, organizations need to adapt quickly or suffer the consequences. To do this requires leadership to be shown throughout an organization. On the other hand, the reality in most organizations is that leadership is concentrated at the top, and certainly authority is concentrated there. I'm now going to explain why this is, and therefore why Ann was right in her comments about modern working life.

We start by moving the focus of the model away from organizational leadership to one of personal leadership. If I want to take responsibility for my life, then I have to display personal leadership in it. So here is my take on personal leadership, using the same model.

Doing: We need to do stuff, otherwise we aren't leading in our lives. Taking action and leading from the front is important if we are to really live. Otherwise, we end up drifting along to nowhere in particular.

Thinking: We need to use our own intellectual capability, to understand what's going on in our lives, and think through potentially complex problems. Otherwise, we may be acting to address the wrong issues.

Being: It's not just about how we think or what we do, effective personal leadership is also about how we are in our work and lives. It is important that we act in line with our own personal values and core purpose. It also covers the need to behave authentically and with integrity rather than putting on a false front, which others would see through sooner or later anyway.

To lead in our own lives means getting the balance right here. However, developments in the modern workplace in the last 40 years have made it more difficult for us to take leadership in our own lives, in two key ways. To illustrate this, let's return to the coal mining father.

The Coal Miner 40 Years Ago

Life, for him, was pretty clear-cut. He had a clear set of rules to work to. He was paid to mine coal. He was told what to do, and when to do it. He had little input into the thinking behind the operation. He could also *be* whatever he wanted, as long as he didn't go telling his supervisor to get lost, in which case he might be in trouble. Within limits, he was able to be himself, to joke around, and to say what he thought about things.

As I say, life was pretty simple. He was paid to do, he wasn't expected to think much, and being was not a work issue at all.

None of this is the case nowadays, and the fascinating thing is that most people see the change intellectually as a good thing. However, that good thing carries potential consequences for us if we're not careful.

The Thinking Explosion

I worked in a manufacturing plant during the 1990s, which at the time was going through significant change to its working practices.

Gone was the idea that workers left their brains at the gate when they came to work. Employees were increasingly expected to think about their jobs, to identify ways to do it better, and to take action to make improvements at work. For people to be empowered in this way, managers needed to relax the previously strong command and control culture that existed. Managers were no longer expected to know everything.

The employer in question was one of the more principled employers I've worked for. I believe their senior managers were genuine in their intentions, even if they found it hard to modify how they behaved on a daily basis. However, I have seen a wide variety of businesses down the years, and when it comes to thinking at work, I believe the only thing that has really changed is where the control culture comes into play. In the old days, the control was to prevent employees from thinking at their work. Now, the control is about controlling *how* people think about their work.

In other words, we are encouraged to think in particular ways. And those particular ways may not be suited to our natural style of thinking.

There is a law of convergence in workplaces (as there is in any organization with groups of people). This law means that, over time and even with no intention at the start, people will tend to converge in their thinking styles. Some types of thinking will become encouraged, while other types won't be—and may be actively penalized. It doesn't even need a senior manager to define how thinking should evolve, though sometimes that is how it happens. In this context, anyone with a different thinking style who goes public too often will gain a reputation as a maverick or worse. If it continues further, the individual is likely to be rejected by the team, perhaps literally, as they leave the organization.

It matters not what the thinking style is. Some organizations encourage creative, expansive styles, like the leading-edge IT companies, while others demand risk-averse, analytical styles. It is clear that, on balance most organizations encourage primarily left brain thinking, with a focus on analysis, argument, and counterargument, rather than the right brain creative thinking styles. That might explain why many creative people struggle to make progress in the workplace. The key point is that some types of thought will be encouraged and other types discouraged.

In extreme cases, I've seen decisions taken in business meetings where most of the meeting participants after the event disagreed with what was decided. Yet, in the meeting itself, they went along with the dominant orthodoxy. We also see this highlighted in the case of whistle blowers, particularly in organizations that went on to fail. The cases at Enron, Vivendi, Northern Rock, Lehman Brothers, and RBS all illustrate this point, when people who did see what was happening voiced their concerns. Such different thinking was not acceptable, and their voice cost them their jobs, even if posterity vindicated their judgment.

Thinking is personal, and proscribing it takes away part of our identity, forcing us to put a thinking mask on, adding it to all the other masks we need at work. But there is one more mask to talk about, and the next one is even more personal.

The Being Journey

It was 1986 when I started out on my career. While I don't really like to admit it, there is much that has changed since I first put a suit on, and joined the London commuter belt near the time of the Stock Market Big Bang. One thing that has changed during that time is the emphasis nowadays on corporate visions, missions, values, and behaviors. They largely didn't exist when I set out on my journey, but there are few organizations that don't have these things in place now.

A lot could be said here about the quality of vision and values statements that are posted on the walls of organizations, offices, and factories in the present era. Much of what I've seen could be summed up as *anodyne*. In my more cynical days, before I discovered personal development, I used to go to the Dilbert[1] [5] website regularly. There, you could download a random mission statement full of meaningless jargon. These downloaded statements didn't look all that different from many mission statements I came across in the real world! Just for entertainment, I have reproduced three random mission statements below.

- It is our job to continually foster world-class infrastructures as well as to quickly create principle-centered sources to meet our customer's needs.

---

[1] It's worth noting that the random mission statement generator is no longer available from this website. However, there are many others available online.

- We will strive to expedite distributed knowledge management with dynamic progress for the benefit of our market and other interested parties.
- We have committed to collaboratively and professionally create value-added and cutting-edge services to provide solutions for our partners.

In some cases, mission statements are organization wide, and imposed from the top. In other cases, there is a degree of consultation on the content, and every team might even have a mission statement of its own. It doesn't matter either way when it comes to wearing masks. In a similar vein, we are expected to display a set of organization-approved behaviors and values in the way we do our jobs.

When it comes to challenging our personal identity, the adoption of collective values and approved behaviors offers a more serious challenge. Their impact is more personal than that of missions, which as we've seen, can simply be irrelevant and amusing. Once we hit the values and behaviors connection, we're dealing with how people are at work, as well as how they think. Organizations are becoming more sophisticated in their use of recruitment tools and psychometric questionnaires to identify people with the requisite behaviors to do the job.

In some cases, they arguably use the recruitment tools too well. One business I came across, when we checked using one well-known personality profile tool, showed 14 out of 17 team members as having identical profiles. It was no surprise that this team displayed a number of blind spots in the way they thought and approached issues, and the mavericks were singled out and at times ridiculed. One irony then is that, as we've become more sophisticated in our use of tools in recruiting and developing people, the result has been to make more systematic the group discrimination that probably happened anyway. In the above example, the team manager managed to achieve that result without the use of psychometric or personality questionnaires. Indeed, he actually objected to the use of psychometric questionnaires because he didn't want to recruit clones into the team!

Of course, some corporate values and approved behaviors can have the same impact as the mission statements, in that they can be amusing or irrelevant. For some examples of this, look no further than here:

> At the essence of the company stands its core values: Colleagues, Customers, Company, and Community. We invite and encourage every colleague to live these values—what we call "standing in the circle." In doing so, we can fulfill our mission of becoming the most admired card and lending business in the world.

What does this actually mean?

One tobacco company had two quite stunning approved corporate behaviors. The first was *Executing with Quality* (yes, I'm not joking!). It stated "we believe in executing with quality by understanding and responding to our companies' adult tobacco consumers' preferences." The second was *Sharing with others*, which goes like "we believe in sharing with others, unleashing the tremendous resources of our people as a force for good into the communities in which we live and work." Sounds more like a messianic philanthropist talking, rather than a tobacco company.

The previously mentioned corporate failure, Enron, proudly trumpeted its core values as being *communication, respect, integrity, and excellence*. The corporate failure did not back this up!

Another corporate failure, this time in banking, talked about *Communication and influencing skills* as a key competency. The definition was:

> Expresses ideas and information accurately and clearly, both orally and in written form, and appreciates the target audience. Selects appropriate styles and content and uses persuasive techniques as appropriate to influence business decisions.

It might just be me, but this is hardly expressed in an inspiring way!

*

Two further points need to be made about the tendency to focus increasingly on individual and team behavior at work. The first point relates primarily to individuals and the way they are viewed in the workplace. In my experience, most of that focus is negative in nature. It is rare for an employee to be praised for doing things the right way, with the primary focus on their strengths. It is much more common for them to be criti-cized, with a focus on their weaknesses.

Appraisal interviews often reflect this bias, with the praise sandwich becoming the shit sandwich in the ears of most employees. The idea of the sandwich is that, if I am underperforming in some way, I will be praised at the start, criticized in the middle, and praised at the end by my manager. That's what managers' appraisal training tells them to do, to soften the blow of criticism. Employees often assume, not at times with-out justification, that the praise has been dredged up so the criticism can be given—and as anyone who likes their lunch will know, it's the filling in the sandwich that matters.

To illustrate this point, step forward the manager who decided to use the praise sandwich to deliver his criticism of a team leader who he thought had failed to train his staff adequately. His praise sandwich for the team leader comprised the following statements.

- The bread—"I like the fact you're always in work on time."
- The filling—"Your staff aren't well enough trained, and it's your job to get it done."
- The bread—"That's a nice tie you have on."

Suffice to say that the rest of the conversation did not go very well!

Similarly, when considering their own learning needs, employees are encouraged to focus on their weaknesses. Much discussion is weakness focused, rather than looking at how to improve our strengths further, and utilize them better. This weakness focus gives us one main message at work: *you're not OK*. So, if it's not OK to be me, then I'd better start acting like someone else. Once again, it's time for a mask.

The second point relates to the team environment. In most organiza-tions, nowadays, we don't just do jobs. We are also expected to work in teams, in a high-performance team working culture. Yet, there is a body of evidence that such an approach does not work that well.

For one example, go to two U.S. researchers, Harvey Robbins and Michael Finley [6]. They had a go at the idea that teams needed to do ev-erything together as a team in order to generate a high-performance team. They concluded that this wasn't the way to get the best out of people, and organizations should "honour their reluctance to lose their individual identity to the team" (Robbins & Finley, 2000). People don't want to be virtually tied together in teams all the time.

The Thinking, Doing, and Being equation

In summary, the nature of the employment contract has changed in the last 50 years. In the 1960s, it read something like, I do work (that I wouldn't choose to do otherwise) for money. Now it reads differently, I also *think* and *be* (in ways I don't want to) for money, while pretending that I do want to.

This shift has made it more challenging for us to hold on to our own coherent identity. It's no wonder that we have a stress epidemic in the workplace nowadays, with stress being the number one reason for work absence.

The Use of Change

As with society, so it is with work. Organizations are just smaller versions of society anyway, and they behave the same way. Only more so, as most of us don't have a vote on who gets on to the board of directors. Like society, organizations use fear as a tool to drive change, and to manage the expectations of the rest of us downward. Consider the following statements. How many of them have you heard during your working life?

- If we don't cut costs, we won't survive.
- This is a dog eat dog market.
- We must make this change if we want to stay at the top.
- Things cannot stay the same if we want to survive.

Do you remember George Orwell? In his prophetic book *Nineteen Eighty-Four* [7], he portrayed a political structure that survived by leaving the population in fear of some enemy. In Orwell's case, it was fear of the outcome of a never-ending war that Oceania was perpetually involved in, with either Eastasia or Eurasia. So, most people in 1984 put their heads down and hoped not to be noticed.

It is the same with modern work. The competition is demonized. Third world low-cost economies are demonized. Technology is portrayed as in some way inevitable when the reality is that mankind is capable of controlling it should we choose to do so. All of this leaves most of us feeling grateful just to have a job. Hoping for a nice job, or a fulfilling job, may be a step too far.

In fact, talking about change in the workplace is no longer good enough—most people have got used to that word. The buzzword now is *transformation*, which means *big change*. When we all get used to transformations, another word will have to be found that is even bigger. This culture of fear combined with expertise and big words are incentives that encourage us to dim our own lights, and hang on. Maybe one day, we'll open up and give it a go. One day. But for many, that day will never arrive.

During my career, I have observed, been part of, and played an active role in attempts to change some aspect or other of an organization's culture. It might be about empowering people, holding more rigorous performance conversations, encouraging people to be more creative and innovative, or whatever.

But how did an organization's culture evolve to where it is to begin with? Usually, the answer includes the following:

1. People in key positions during history behaved in certain ways, or did certain things, and those things hugely impacted on culture, or *the way we do things around here.* Look no further than the likes of Henry Ford, Bill Gates, or Sir Fred Goodwin. For good, ill, or somewhere in between, the cultures of Ford, Microsoft, and the Royal Bank of Scotland were heavily impacted by these people and the way they behaved.

2. Stories and legends that are told by people, again and again. These stories are of deeds done and things said in the past, at key moments in the organization's history. They shaped what happened, and impacted on culture. Courageous actions, decisions to take the organization in a different direction, and the like were pivotal moments, and the way the story is told down the line makes their impact even greater. The dragon may have been a four-foot midget when it was faced down at the time, but with time and embellishment it soon becomes a 20-foot fire breather.

*

What this says is that culture primarily is the result of individual actions. Indeed, organizational change takes place at a fundamental level due to the actions of key individuals, and not as a result of any planned organization change program.

Gandhi, a key leader of one of the largest organizations in history (India), is reputed to have said that you should "be the change you want to see in the world." He recognized that you could say anything you wanted, and nothing would change. It's what you did that mattered much, much more. He was right then, and those words are still right.

The Bigger Question

The question we should answer is, what do we do if organizational values conflict with our own? Now the answer will usually be either we leave, or we live with it. But what is undeniable is that, in work, businesses see themselves as paying people for aspects of their *being* that would have been unthinkable 50 years ago. If we are required to do things, think and behave in ways that are not our natural ways, how does that affect us?

I reckon Ann answered that question for us. By the end of a working day, we are so tired from putting on these masks that we have little energy left to do much else. We are emotionally and intellectually drained. With these thinking and being developments, we are more fragmented at work than our coal miner could ever have been. No wonder so many people feel disempowered, as Ann did.

All in all, we are under considerable pressure to fragment as human beings, and cover up who we are. Those pressures start in childhood, and always have done. However, trends in society and work have increased this pressure, often through subtle means. We fragment more often, without even noticing that we are doing so.

This trend poses us a big question. If we are fragmenting ourselves in more and more ways, what are the risks of us losing ourselves completely? Fragmentation costs us emotional and intellectual energy, but could it cost us even more than this?

CHAPTER 4

The Consequences of Fragmentation

The great majority of us are required to live a life of constant duplicity. Your health is bound to be affected if, day after day, you say the opposite of what you feel, if you grovel before what you dislike, and rejoice at what brings you nothing but misfortune

—Boris Pasternak

It takes a huge amount of energy to bend ourselves out of shape. To make this point, I'm going to use an analogy. In the TV program series of *Star Trek*, there was a category of alien species that were known as *shape shifters*. As the name implies, they are creatures capable of changing shape, and appearing as different types of beings from their natural state. So, while they might be a green blob in reality, they could appear to us as any other life form for a while.

But eventually these shape shifters had to rest, and when they did they returned to their natural shape. It took a lot of their energy to reshape themselves, and so they needed recovery time afterward.

Where else have you heard that phrase *recovery time* before? I associate it with people crashing out in the evening after work, or with weekends, or holidays. In other words, it's that time where you can relax from the impact of work, and be yourself. That's if you can be yourself in your home life, as many people will feel it necessary to shape shift there too.

It should be no surprise that aging prematurely and health problems are made more likely by living a fragmented life. After all, if you run a car into the ground, bumping it over terrain it is unsuited for, you cannot be surprised when the engine gives up or when things go wrong.

A seminal work on fragmentation was written more than 50 years ago, called *The divided self* by R D Laing [1]. Laing was a psychiatrist, who looked into the nature of mental illness, which he also experienced himself. He came to some startling conclusions, which chime with the idea of masks and fragmentation. One of his contributions was the realization that:

> I would wish to emphasize that our 'normal' 'adjusted' state is too often the abdication of ecstasy, the betrayal of our true potentialities, that many of us are only too successful in acquiring a false self to adapt to false realities. (Laing, 1990)

This makes mental illness essentially a normal response to an insane situation. He observed that children often have to choose between the identity being foisted on them by their parents, and their own personal experience of who they really are. If they choose the former, they give up on who they are. Choose the latter then they risk losing parental approval. Most people end up giving up their own identity and adopting a false one. It is this, believed Laing, which led to some people going mad.

Short of going mad or suffering from depression, there are plenty of other consequences to be borne from living the fragmented life, if indeed it is *lived* at all. Four immediate consequences are outlined below.

Alcohol and Drugs

The beer and wine on a Friday night is fine. But for many, it soon becomes the glass of wine every evening. Every evening, and often it is a big glass. Nor do the drugs have to be recreational ones, though they do count. Many prescription and over-the-counter drugs are taken essentially to ease the pain, either mental or physical, from our bodies as they react badly to being driven over rough ground.

Of course, we are entitled to the odd night out with alcohol. Personally, I have always drawn the line at recreational drugs (might as well get that question out of the way!). But when it becomes a habit, there's a question to be asked. We often drink to escape life, not to live, as so many people think. That's why many people get angry, sad, or weepy when they've had a few drinks. That's the part of themselves that is suppressed in day-to-day life. The effect of alcohol is to lower the masks, and potentially to give an insight into the real person. This doesn't mean the emotions will be expressed appropriately, but at least they are expressed. The rest of the time, we suppress them.

Cynicism

How many people do you know who are cynical, sometimes even when there's no obvious reason to be so? Cynicism can be deployed on people or events that have little or nothing to do with the cynic. But where it does have relevance, this suggests a level of personal fragmentation.

After all, babies and young children aren't born cynical. It is something we develop with age. It develops when the natural idealistic expectations we are born with are dampened down, and our natural approach to life is gradually bent out of shape. Rather than deal with being put out of shape, we become cynical instead.

The Need to Recover

We see evidence of the need to recover all around us. This includes the *Friday syndrome*, accompanied by the opportunity to let our hair down for the weekend (if we have any!). We see it in people who live for holidays, so they can get away from the office, and then crash out for 2 weeks. Personally, I'm always amazed by people who are willing to spend a fortune to go on holiday for 4 weeks a year to recover from the hell that is the other 48 weeks; but who aren't willing to invest even a fraction of that sum to try to improve the other 48 weeks.

Paradoxically, we also see the same issue in reverse with people who live for work. For some people, work may be where they can be most themselves, and it's in other areas of their life where they have to resort to their wardrobe of masks.

When people live for one part of their life, it's a sure sign that fragmentation is a key factor elsewhere.

Absence

In some cases, we will literally be talking about real absence. For example, people being absent from work, or being sick when a big domestic occasion rears its head that they don't want to attend. However, my definition of absent is *not present*. We have many ways to describe this, my favorite one being *the lights are on but there's no one in*. The human spirit is not where the body is. It is preoccupied with past or future, somewhere else. Somewhere else where we need to adopt a role, so of course we have to think about it. That means we aren't thinking or acting on the situation that is right under our nose right now.

*

So far, the signs I have described are immediate signs, in that we can see them in ourselves or others if we look. However, there are three long-term consequences that I want to talk about. All of them are far reaching in their impact on us as human beings.

1. Premature Setting

When I was first introduced to the work of Carl Jung [2], the famous psychologist, I was fascinated by his views on the development of the human personality as we get older.

As I understood his message, we all have our natural personality preferences. Some of us, for example, might prefer to operate in a world that is structured and planned while others might prefer to play things by ear. Another example would be that some people prefer to make decisions with their heart, and others with their head. Some are creative and intuitive, while others prefer the world of analysis. Some of us have strong preferences for particular styles, and others don't. We all have our natural preferences, and however we got them, our preferences carry with them great strength, and some challenges.

However, provided we are living comfortably, there comes a time in most of our lives where we will tend to want to search for completeness. We generally have the desire to become whole in some way. *Whole* in this context means that we can use all of the above preferences sometimes, including our weaker ones. This desire for wholeness often leads initially to the search for a partner. There is plenty of evidence that most people eventually find a partner who is opposite to them; opposites literally do attract! That way, we become whole as a partnership, even if we are not individually whole. This wholeness has a biological function, as to successfully raise children means having to be good at everything.

By contrast, there's also plenty of evidence that opposites attract less well as we get older, partly because we want someone we can agree with more often. But, according to Jung, another factor also comes into play with age. Our desire for *wholeness* becomes more personal, and cannot be satisfied by being with someone who is good at the things we're not.

This desire for personal wholeness might show itself in an accountant, for example, whose job involves lots of structure, planning, and analysis. Accountancy is a career path suited to the analytical part of our brain. However, our accountant might suddenly discover an interest in painting at age 40. This allows them to develop a previously underused part of the brain, and allow it to flourish. It is an attempt to display the full range of human potential, a potential we all have. Part of the midlife crisis syndrome we all talk about is motivated by this search for wholeness. Where this desire is not addressed earlier, it often results in crisis or apparently random events, like a sudden decision to emigrate, a complete change of career, or a sudden change of life partner. Even the purchase of that symbol of (mainly) male desperation, the sports car, can be a sign of this.

In my time, I've seen this level of change occur regularly. I've known marketing managers discover an interest in forensic science. I've seen business executives do charitable work. I've seen the most sociable and outgoing people suddenly deciding to go off to a retreat, where they didn't talk for days. These are all very different activities from each other, and all utilizing different parts of our brain and personality.

But what happens if for some reason, we elect not to do this, or are prevented from doing this self-development? The answer, according to Jung, is that we effectively become more of a caricature as we age. We get old instead of grow old. Our strongest personality traits become stronger and stronger, while our weaker ones gradually wither and die. Literally, what doesn't get used gets lost. We see this most visibly in people who appear to become set in their ways as they age. Premature setting is the term I use to refer to this when it occurs.

In this case, our accountant will dismiss any interests or opportunities that might develop different talents, perhaps scorning art as a waste of time. The analytical, detail conscious brain becomes stronger still, and even in retirement days will be planned out in military detail days in advance, if not weeks. They might become hard to live with. The idea of doing anything spontaneous would be a nonstarter, unless time was budgeted for it, say a couple of hours next Tuesday!

In short, as we become older, we either develop our latent potential as human beings and move into an exciting fourth dimension, or we become two-dimensional or even one-dimensional. Which option would you rather take?

Jung's conclusions are fascinating when we combine them with how we tend to fragment ourselves to cope with modern life. Essentially when we fragment, we split ourselves to some extent into different people for different parts of our lives. As we put our masks on, we set ourselves into certain molds. If they are set in large numbers and early in life, we are caught unable to develop our latent potential, as doing this means changing the molds. The result of this is that our personality sets prematurely. We are caught in the situation where we don't develop, so the two- or one-dimensional me might be all that's left by the end.

We reach the end of our life, and what might have been is only might have been. What sort of an ending is that? Mask and mold yourself too much, and the chances are high that the ending could be like this.

Putting on all these masks and roles has another consequence, which is linked to the above one. It is just as serious.

2. We Lose Sight of Who We Are

Many people are pushed out of shape so far and so frequently that they risk losing sight of their real self. If we never act out who we really are, then how do we know? We put on roles so often that we become them. Our real self is lost in a world of roles, pressures, and expectations generated by ourselves and other people. This is a miserable outcome. We might do lots of things, think lots of things, and even be popular with other people. But that isn't us. Would we have wanted those goals if we could choose them? Would we even have wanted those friends?

I am surprised at how often I encounter this bleak result. Jennifer was in her late forties, and as so often the case, she looked outwardly successful, and put on a good act for others. That act disguised a history of depression, and as it turns out, the descent into another one. Jennifer was immersed in the importance of keeping up appearances. She held down a senior job, working for a prestigious boss on a high salary. She was married, though her relationship was under immense strain. Her family relationships were strained, particularly with her younger sister, who also put a high premium on keeping up appearances. This led to sibling rivalry on who could keep up the best appearance. Many of her friendships were superficial, but they all had to be kept going. Jennifer was very critical of her friends behind their back, but would not let this out when in front of them.

Holidays for Jennifer served two functions. They provided rest and re-spite from a life of imagery. But they also formed a status symbol of their own: exotic holidays could be used as a sign of success after all. She clung to the idea that she had been raised from a working-class family, and had made good. This was one of the most powerful masks in her wardrobe, and it dominated much of her life.

Ironically, when the pressure was off, it was the simple things that Jennifer enjoyed most—nature, flowers, and the countryside. Underneath all the masks, she had a playful nature. These pleasures were fleeting events for Jennifer, as "life is not like that. It is full of hard knocks."

In Jennifer's case, her identity had been burdened with so many outfits that it had simply chosen to walk away. What if that happens to us too?

With all our masks and outfits covering up the real me, the one thing we are guaranteed not to be is one of the latest buzzwords in Western society. Being authentic is virtually impossible to achieve.

3. We Cannot Behave Authentically

We hear a lot about authenticity nowadays, particularly in the workplace and especially when talking about leaders. We all want to believe we're authentic ourselves, and we all want to be led by authentic people. One of the areas I coach people in is leadership, and authenticity is one of the main topics that gets talked about. From my experience in organizations, and my observations of society, I have noticed the following two statements as generally true.

1. The more often that someone talks of authenticity or postures as an authentic leader, the less authentic I experience them to be.
2. When people talk about authenticity, they usually refer to other people and not to themselves. The primary focus is on what we want from others.

Authenticity is like honesty and discretion. If we are genuinely these things, we don't need to say it. Everyone else will know that we have these qualities.

The key to being authentic is simple. We cannot be truly authentic without being ourselves, and we cannot be ourselves without having a coherent personal identity. Fragmentation is bad news then, because if we are fragmented we cannot be authentic, and we will not be perceived as authentic. If we're not being authentic, then sooner or later, other people are going to notice. In the meantime, deep down, we will know it anyway.

Of course, there are skills and techniques you can give someone to enable them to appear more authentic. That's why many political and business leaders go to school or get a coach to learn the techniques. A warm smile here, a handshake there, good eye contact, and the world's your oyster.

That approach might work up to a point. But sooner or later, the facade is exposed. Tony Blair, the former British Prime Minister, illustrates the point. When he first took office, we saw behavior that looked and seemed engaging; "hi, I'm Tone" being a famous self-introduction he once made, that gave the impression of being a man of the people, everybody's friend. He consulted, he listened, and he looked concerned when people spoke to him. But it was eventually exposed as false, most notably by the Iraq war. In this case, he ignored the biggest demonstration of public opinion in Britain's history.

I've experienced the false authentic in business too. The leader who manages to manufacture the false smile, and who engages in false consultation when they've already made their mind up. Sooner or later, they get found out. We've all met them, people who move on regularly before their mistakes catch up with them. Often, they end up at the senior end of businesses and organizations!

A more light-hearted example of this was a senior manager in a manufacturing company. Simon used to love being able to pass on snippets of information to those who worked for him, his catchphrase being "don't tell anyone else about this, but . . ." He would then go on to tell you something. Simon was effectively asking you to keep something confidential when he wasn't doing so himself. He wasn't practicing what he preached, and the consequences of this were obvious. The people he told in turn let on to other people. The embarrassment was palpable on one occasion when he went public on something he thought no one else knew about. It soon became clear that everybody else knew already!

I used to be jealous when I saw inauthentic managers being outwardly successful despite their lack of authenticity. But now I'm not jealous at all. Why the change of view? One clue lies in the surveys carried out into the fears of top managers in organizations. The biggest fear that gets consistently expressed is the fear of being *found out*. The implication is that most senior managers, deep down, don't think they're doing that good a job, and eventually they will be rumbled by others—and lose their jobs as a result.

A term has been coined for outwardly successful people who feel inadequate inside: imposter syndrome. This phenomenon was first identified by clinical psychologists Pauline Clance and Suzanne Imes in 1978, in a study that first looked at its impact on women in particular [3]. The irony of imposter syndrome is that the more outwardly successful you become, the greater the gap between what you've outwardly achieved and how you feel, and the worse the fear becomes.

If I'm a senior manager and being found out is my biggest fear, then that suggests I feel inadequate about myself. What a lonely place to feel inadequate, when you're a senior manager. If that is how we feel, we cannot behave authentically. The only thing we can do is to put on the mask and go on the stage. But, behind that mask, the nagging doubt goes on.

The conclusion from all this is obvious. We cannot be authentic if we have wardrobes full of masks. To be authentic means being true to ourselves, and we can't do that if we don't even know who we are. True authenticity, as opposed to surface authenticity, requires personal coherence.

We will go on to look at a model for doing this in part 2 of the book. But first, there are a number of responses to fragmentation that involve personal development to some degree, which I believe fail to deal with the issue. In other words, they are avoidance strategies. Let's have a look at some of these before we move on to deal with how we do address fragmentation.

CHAPTER 5

Some Responses to Fragmentation

Insanity in individuals is something rare – but in groups, nations, parties and epochs, it is the rule.

—Friedrich Nietzsche

We are experiencing a fragmentation epidemic in the Western world. When we face a personal crisis, we often find ourselves asking fundamental questions about our identity and the purpose of life. In the midst of this epidemic, I have noticed five common strategies for trying to deal with these questions that appear to be gaining in popularity. These strategies are attempts to give ourselves a sense of our own unique personal identity, and to establish our purpose.

The first strategy involves going back to the past, our origins. The second involves fast-forwarding to the future, and where we will end up. The third puts its prime focus on being positive. The fourth involves relying on therapy and personal development, and the final one puts the acquisition of money center stage.

In this chapter, I will outline each of these strategies. While they all have something to recommend them, they each come up short as a strategy to *find yourself*, for reasons I will go on to explain.

The First Strategy: Back to the Past

The retreat to the past is about genealogy. It is an attempt to find our identity by going back to our own ancestry, answering the question, where did

I come from? We research our own family tree, and if we are lucky, we may be able to go back hundreds of years and many generations. It is also a great way of reconnecting with family members we may have lost touch with, which can be comforting on its own.

In this way, we discover who was connected to whom, where the generational skeletons are in the family cupboards, what it is that different people did for a living, and where in the world different branches of our family came from.

This last piece of information seems to give us particularly strong identities. As the joke goes, there are about 800 million Irish people in the world, judging by those who claim Irish ancestry! Behind this, there is great desire to find our identity from the past, and then to embrace it. We may also hold onto family traits and professions, for example *we're an army family*, or *we've always had a great sense of fun!* We may indeed have a genetic disposition to behave in certain ways, or to do certain things. However, this does not make us who we are. Our personal identity is different from this; it is unique to each of us.

Some of us may be genuinely interested in our family history out of curiosity, and there is nothing wrong with that. However, finding this information will not resolve the life issues we face right now. It won't reduce our fragmentation levels. It won't make us feel better, and it won't cure that nagging feeling that something isn't right. That feeling won't go away.

The Second Strategy: Back to the Future

This isn't a remake of the Marty McFly movie of 1980s fame. Instead, it describes a second tendency I've noticed. How many people do you know, that when they go through a major crisis, suddenly start to develop an interest in the future, particularly through religion and spirituality? It's almost as if we have to develop an understanding of where we go after death to make any sense of this life here right now.

Our religious and spiritual investigation takes off, and we try to gain our identity from the future. After all, if we know where we're going (or at least develop some faith about where we're going) then we can work out why we're here, or what we're here to do. This can, in extreme cases (often with people low in self-esteem) end up in cults being joined, where the person's identity simply becomes that of the cult, and their purpose becomes one of serving the cult.

Trying to gain a sense of self-identity through this route won't work any more successfully than the genealogy route. Again, I am not saying that exploring religion and spiritual beliefs is not a worthwhile pursuit. But it won't help you get a meaningful self-identity.

In the 19th century, Karl Marx [1] was famously misquoted as describing religion as *the opiate of the people*. By this, he meant that the promise of a better life after death was held out as the reward for putting up with an intolerable life right now. At that time, life for many workers in Western Europe was pretty miserable, in Victorian factories and mills.

In those days, working conditions had a major impact on this misery. In a different way, life for many now has become intolerable due to the impact on the self and our loss of identity. So it is in the same way that spirituality can become the opiate of the people, the means to come to terms with who we really are. Unfortunately, it just doesn't work. Finding our purpose from trying to connect to spirit or to source is futile when we can't even connect with ourselves properly. When we use religion or spirituality as a substitute for sorting out our own problems, it will fail as a strategy. We still need to take action ourselves in our own world, right here, right now.

The Third Strategy: Retreat to the Positive

This strategy is less about trying to discover our true identity, and more about trying to reinvent one for ourselves. It is to the land of the positive we go!

This approach holds that the key to happiness and prosperity is to think positively, and you will get positive results. It also translates the message into an urge not to engage in any negative thinking at all. Negative thought and emotions will translate into bad results. The implication of this approach is that we suppress and ignore any negative thinking and only think, and talk, positively. The law of attraction and the ideas around unconditional positive regard contain a similar approach.

Much has been written about the importance of being positive. The idea that if you view life through an optimistic lens, not only are things more likely to turn out well, but you will feel better. The *glass half full* mentality does serve people well. In contrast, it is equally clear that viewing life through a negative lens can cause depression, and can certainly reinforce one.

So positive thinking is good then, but is it unconditionally good? Should we always be positive? I would argue that remaining unconditionally positive carries consequences for your health, relationships, and life. Let's explore these consequences briefly.

1. Your Health

There are a number of studies that have been done into the relationship between your outlook on life and your health. Broadly speaking, people were placed into categories, defined according to how they viewed life and the events and challenges encountered during it. The results are rather interesting.

We would generally expect negative people to suffer the worst health issues, and this is indeed the case. Of course, they might argue that they wouldn't be as negative if they were healthier! But generally speaking, *glass half empty* people are less healthy than more optimistic types.

However, there is a twist in this tale. Another group of people who apparently suffer from poorer than average health are those who always view and talk about life in positive terms. What's that all about? Here's my take on why this happens. The people in this group would be what I call *false positives*. They are so because they have a deep held belief in not saying negative things, about self, others, or anything. They don't allow themselves the luxury of a bad day, they avoid confronting issues, and they don't recognize or release negative feelings. Over time, this suppression creates health time bombs that if left for long enough, go off inside us. What your heart and mind doesn't recognize and your mouth doesn't say will be pushed down inside your body, to be channeled into stress and illness. Maybe even death.

I talk from some experience, having had a couple of health scares myself. Getting old stuff off our chest is a great thing to do for our health. From my personal experience, I've seen too many nice people die early, of cancer and other health issues. So bottling things up and choosing not to recognize bad situations where they occur won't serve us well.

The healthiest group is what I'd term the *realistically positive*, those who generally view life through a positive lens. But when things aren't going well, they let it out, and let others know. Hopefully they do so without alienating other people. In other words, they emphasize the positive, but don't ignore the negative.

2. Your Relationships

False positives are often not great to have around. Not only do they appear as inauthentic or false, but they create stress in people they come into contact with. Here's an example to illustrate how that happens.

I used to know a manager who was unconditionally positive, and he was generally a nice guy. But he avoided confrontation as a religion. One day, he walked into the office just as two professional staff were cooling down from a heated argument. I had become involved, and to say there was an atmosphere of tension in the office would be a massive understatement. Anyway, at this time, the aforementioned manager walked in, looked around, smiled, and uttered the immortal words "isn't it great to see so much talent in this room!" So much for a positive outlook helping the situation. Most of us could have cheerfully throttled him, and his intervention resulted in the stress levels rising further.

False positivity and perceived insincerity go closely together.

3. Your Life

Being a false positive is bad for your life. Why do I say this? I remember Steve Nobel, a personal development speaker, talking a few years back about how we can grow through inspiration or as a result of desperation. This insight has stuck with me over the years. However, an analysis of why people change highlights that, for most people, the desperation element has a stronger motivating force in change. That's why change most often takes place in response to a crisis—be it a change of career, collapse in a relationship, or a company taking emergency measures to survive. Vision and inspiration on their own are not enough. Even visionary leaders, like Nelson Mandela, started from a position of desperation.

Ask yourself the question: What prompted your last significant life change? Most people will answer in a way that includes an element of crisis.

Viewing everything in *good* terms is a guaranteed way of never making the changes you need to make. Problems become opportunities or challenges, no one and nothing is bad, and smiling is mandatory. There's only one problem when it comes to this and personal identity. The problem is that we are choosing to ignore a whole side of our being, the side that is grizzly, grumpy, and negative. This will simply not do. Yet a whole flotilla of thinking has grown up around the idea that you must never be negative.

Negative things are present in the universe. Without electrons, charged negative particles, there would be no life. The universe would not hang together. But we conveniently ignore this when it comes to our psyche. It's not OK to have a negative thought, so we have only positive ones because we want to be OK. If we think too negatively too often, why we may be encouraged to go to a therapist! Real positive thinking is about finding a way forward that's compatible with the *real you*. It's not about pretending how wonderful the earthquake was.

In summary, the retreat to the positive is itself a mask, which if anything, increases our degree of personal fragmentation. Being falsely positive comes across as inauthentic precisely because it is inauthentic. If we are wearing a mask, we cannot be authentic. We're also denying a significant part of who we are, and that cannot be a good thing either.

One countercurrent writer on positive thinking in recent years is Oliver Burkeman [2]. He argues that, not only is the positive movement itself flawed, but the single-minded pursuit of happiness is also flawed. In fact, the very act of pursuing happiness makes it less likely that you will find it. Burkeman advocates what he calls the "negative path to happiness" (Burkeman, 2012). He exposes the futility of a purely positive approach by highlighting the point that anyone who has resolved to think positive in future then has to monitor their own mind to make sure they never have a negative thought. In other words, trying to banish negative thinking ends up having the thinker's mind focused on negative thoughts!

The Fourth Strategy: Personal Development or Therapy

This sounds like, and often is, a positive move in terms of dealing with the wardrobe of masks we may have. However, this strategy also has potential pitfalls. The first can be seen in the serial therapy student. How many people do you know who like nothing better than to be in a good mess? I've known quite a few in my time.

It's a variation of the wartime cry that what we need right now is a crisis! Therapy, and the need for it, becomes that crisis; it becomes another mask to put on. Good therapists are on the lookout for this, but of course not all therapists are good. What's more, some patients are very skilled at putting the mask on in the first place. This is ironic, because many people who find a way forward in therapy go in with the intention of finding out more about themselves, and to discover a happier future.

I remember going to hear the Dalai Lama give a talk in 2004. His key message that day was that "everyone has the right to live a happy life." It was perhaps a surprise coming from someone whose country was invaded and occupied when he was barely out of childhood, more than 50 years before. His words, his simple message, resonated strongly with me then. It still does.

Happiness is an issue for our time, with record numbers of people registering discontent or even depression. Amidst all this, the road to happiness appears to be littered with potholes.

I have observed down the years that there are many people who seem to be in serial personal development or therapy, who don't look very happy. Isn't that obvious, I hear you say? After all, one key stimulus that leads us into a personal development journey to begin with is the sense of discontent with where we are. By implication, life has to become fairly intolerable before some of us are willing to make a change. That is a fair enough point.

But what about those who are on this journey, have been on it for many years (even decades), and still don't look happy? A few years ago, I worked with a group of people who were passionate about self-development, and pursued it to great depth professionally. Yet, when I looked around, I saw people surrounded by dysfunctional lives and generally unhappy in their demeanor. Many among their number were in therapy, some of them long term. Yet the golden chalice of happiness was out of reach. It was out of reach for me, too, because I ended up seeing a therapist myself!

Now, before I move on with this story, I must point out that my experience in therapy was transformational, and many aspects of my life began to shift for the better as a result. So, personal development and therapy do have transformative properties. But why do so many personal developers and therapists seem unhappy? Why are so many people out there pursuing happiness and failing to achieve it?

For me, the answer comes down to one issue—there is a limit to the extent we should focus on our own self, and our past. During the above period in my life, I spent a lot of time in self-reflection. This concentrated both on my own personality, and on the past that I saw as turning me into who I'd become. My focus was on me and my past. Some of that focus can be helpful, in clearing debris from the past and becoming more self-aware. However, too much focus on self and past is like too much salt in your diet: salt is vital to healthy functioning, but too much of it is undoubtedly *bad* for us. It is the same with historical self-absorption.

If this focus doesn't lead to a happy life, what does?

The answer is the very opposite of historical self-absorption. The key to moving toward a happier state contains two elements.

1. A Focus on the Future

I don't mean focus on the future to the exclusion of the present; the present is the only bit of time we can affect. But looking for ways to move forward to a positive future, and taking action with that as the objective will reap dividends. Yes, unpick whatever you need to from the past if it's preventing you from moving forward, and learn from past mistakes and events. But otherwise leave the past well alone, and cease the tendency to self-ruminate.

In the end, we can't change the past. We can only change the future by acting differently in the present.

2. A Focus on Other People

If self-absorption is a bad idea, focusing on other people is one of the key ways to find happiness. For a start, you become a nicer person to be around because you're interested in other people on their terms, not yours. *Serve others* as a mantra is ironic, as it is the best way to create a greater sense of personal fulfillment. You take yourself out of your own head, and put it to the service of others. Besides, the feeling that we are in some way making a difference to others is one that most of us want to have.

The conclusion from this is clear. If happiness is what you want, start creating it instead of investigating why you weren't happy in the first place. Live in the present rather than spending your life in personal development and therapy, with no end in sight.

The Fifth Strategy: Forward to a Fortune!

It is ironic that we follow a discussion on happiness with a discussion about money. Many of you will know about one of the iconic books of the recent self-help movement, *The Secret* [3]. This is but one example of the forward to a fortune approach. This book, with its accompanying CDs and DVD, has sparked a movement of followers. While many movements down the years begin with a grain of truth, it usually gets followed by a load of propaganda that followers are expected to embrace.

In the *Secret's* case, the grain of truth is rather straightforward (as truth usually is). To paraphrase the Henry Ford maxim, "whether you believe you can, or that you can't, you're right." In other words, your expectations play a major part in your success or failure. *The Secret* develops ideas around the law of attraction, that we attract what we expect to attract, whether we want it or not.

I have three reasons why this approach should at the very least be taken with reservations.

Reason 1: It Takes the Help Out of Self-Help

Core to this approach is the idea that if you visualize yourself as successful, you will be successful. This is encapsulated by the mantra employed throughout—*thoughts become things*. What does that mean? Well, to take it to its extreme, if you sit eating a three-course meal, then lay on the couch dreaming yourself fitting a pair of tight fitting jeans, you will fit those jeans someday soon. You will be putting out a signal to the universe that goes something like *me slim, me slim, me slim*. As Ali Baba would say, open sesame, you will be slim. The universe will make it so.

Unfortunately, just visualizing yourself achieving success is not enough on its own. You must also take action.

Reason 2: It Equates Wealth with Happiness

Pretty well every contributor to this book has a number of key things in common.

1. They are rich, or at least comfortable.
2. Their primary focus appears to be on creating financial wealth, and
3. They seem to equate money with happiness.

What happened to companionship, spiritual development, making a wider contribution to society, health, families, and all the other things that make life worth living? While these things are mentioned now and again, the overwhelming emphasis is on wealth creation.

When I read *The Secret*, it came across to me as a sermon by the rich for the less rich about how they got rich. All they did, of course, was to visualize themselves being rich. One interesting question is posed for us to consider: What is it that the richest one percent has that you don't that made them that way? (Apart from the obvious answer, money!)

Now, the response they were seeking was *they think they will generate money, so they do*. However, what about the many other answers—advantage of birth, use of power, being a brilliant inventor or businessperson, inherited money, having rich parents, and having a good education. All of these elements are relevant, and all are ignored by this approach.

My third reason for treating the law of attraction with caution is the least obvious. But it is also potentially the most dangerous.

Reason 3: It's Your Fault You're Miserable!

If the well-off and contented are getting what they visualize, then it is also true that the badly off and unhappy are also getting what they visualize. The homeless, the unemployed, and the depressed are all that way due to how they think.

Let's take it to the next level. Just consider the poor and starving in Africa, those dying as the result of natural disasters, and the Holocaust victims in the 1940s. Did they all bring this upon themselves through the way they visualized, and their failure to see a good outcome? I say it in those shocking terms to bring to light the danger behind such thinking.

We don't just live in a world where each of us as individuals can shape our own destiny, independently of everybody else. Clearly, we are impacted greatly by the thoughts and attitudes of other people, particularly by those who are immediately around us. If this wasn't the case, why do we have so many masks to wear? The only reason we end up wearing them is the power of the community we are part of at any point in time.

The irony is that pursuing that fortune won't make you feel good. Money is intrinsically worthless, and that is a metaphor for how our own lives end up when we make money the God we pursue. We end up with a life that is intrinsically worthless.

*

If the above strategies fall short, what will work?

The road to personal coherence is not a new one, although some of the modern pressures are new. In 1961, Carl Rogers [4] documented his observations of what his own psychotherapy clients went through as they received treatment for their disorders. As clients moved to pull their lives back together, he observed some interesting trends in what they did.

- They moved away from facades, of pretending to be someone they weren't.
- They stopped worrying about what they *ought* to do or be like.
- They stopped automatically worrying about whether they were meeting the expectations of other people, or of needing to please other people.
- They moved toward self-direction, becoming more autonomous in making life choices and accepting the consequences of them.
- They became more accepting of other people. (Rogers, 1961)

As we will see, becoming more coherent (and so less fragmented) will involve all of these elements. The question we face now, of course, is how do we get there?

To Conclude

Many people set out at some point in their life on a quest to find themselves. However, using the five strategies mentioned in this chapter won't achieve that. Instead, they either deny the issue of fragmentation, or they increase it by encouraging mask wearing.

OK, I hear you say, so how do I become a whole person? How do I find the *real me*? The first step is to consider where you currently are. How fragmented are you? In the next chapter, you will have the chance to answer this question for yourself.

PART 2

The Road to Personal Coherence

CHAPTER 6

How Coherent Am I Right Now?

Those are my principles. If you don't like them, I have others.
—Groucho Marx

The first step to personal coherence is to assess the extent to which you are fragmented in the first place. In this chapter, I'm going to ask you to do a bit of self-assessment. You may wish to refer back to the answers you gave to some self-assessment questions in chapter 2 of this book.

To remind yourself of what a fragmented personal identity looks like, you might want to refer back to the case studies of Jackie in chapter 2, and Jennifer in chapter 4. Jackie and Jennifer, in their own unique ways, were dominated by masks that were geared up to meet the expectations of other people, and to impress them. Both ended up living lives that were not their own.

Exercise: The Wheel of Life

The Wheel of life is a simple idea, but applying it can produce powerful and revealing results. Our life can be divided into a number of key areas—career, finances, family, health, and so on. In principle, the happier we are with a particular part of our life, the more likely it is that we're being ourselves in that area. The opposite is also true: the more masks we put on, the less happy we're likely to be. In this exercise, you will survey your general happiness across the whole of your life.

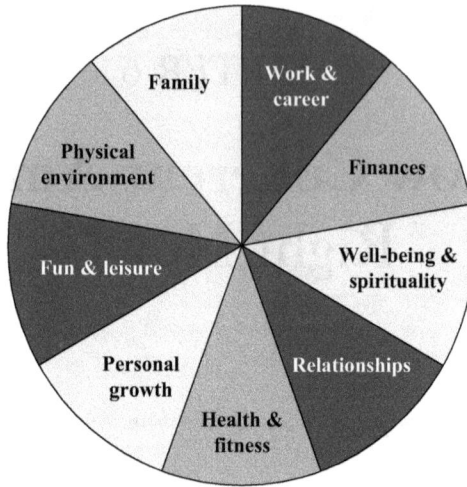

Figure 6.1 Wheel of life: example

There are three steps to carrying out the Wheel of life exercise.

Step 1 is to divide your life up into its key areas. A typical Wheel of life looks like Figure 6.1 above. You can either use the same headings, or draw a wheel with the headings that represent the important elements in your own life.

For many of you, the above headings will generally fit. Whether you choose to use these headings or not, most people will identify between 8 and 10 key areas in their life.

Step 2 is to score each segment of the wheel from 1 to 10. A score of 1 means this segment feels awful right now. A score of 10 means you are completely satisfied with how it is going. In scoring each segment, the question you are answering is *how do I feel about my life in this area?* At this stage, you do not need to justify your score, just go with how you feel overall for that area.

Step 3 is to do some analysis behind the scores. Why have you scored each segment the way you have? What reasons can you see for any low scores? Where you have scored high, why are they high? How could you improve your scores in the future? Once you have completed these steps, you have an across your life picture of how happy or unhappy you are. This in turn gives you some potential areas to focus on with regard to how fragmented you are.

Now consider the following questions, answering them as best you can for yourself.

1. Which part of my Wheel of life gives me most cause for concern?
2. In what ways am I being bent out of shape here? What or who by?
3. Where do I most see the *real me* coming out to play?
4. Is there any part of my wheel where I might be in denial? If so, which part?

To help with this last question, consider the five signs of dis-ease that come into play when we are fragmented. If you remember from chapter 4, they were alcohol and drugs, depression, cynicism, the need for recovery time, and absence.

- In which areas of your life do these come into play for you?
- What is it that triggers them?
- Which of these five signs is the one that is most present in your life?
- What light does this throw onto the results in your Wheel of life?

Finally, based on the above exercise, which areas of your life do you want to do something about?

The Road to Personal Coherence

Having diagnosed your current levels of fragmentation, I will now introduce the model I plan to work with for the rest of this book. It is a powerful way to increase our personal coherence, a concrete self-identity that we can build on in our lives. The model enables you to answer four questions about yourself. The questions are:

1. What is my inner voice saying to me?
2. How do I regain my own self-belief?
3. What is it I'm really about? and
4. How can I learn to express myself authentically?

Applying this model rigorously will work, and I can say that personally. It is not always an easy model to follow, but it is a simple one. Applying it will involve challenging yourself, and at times other people. It will mean taking a few risks along the way. At each stage, and with each of the questions, I will show you techniques and approaches that work for me, and for many other people I've coached.

The alternative is to play it safe, but still feel insecure. The alternative is to keep the masks on. To bathe in our own continuing unworthiness. To hope that someday, in some way, we will feel better.

I don't think that approach works. There are millions of elderly people sitting out there with lots of regrets. This is your opportunity to not be one of them.

Let's take the first step on the journey then, and locate that inner voice of yours.

CHAPTER 7

What Is My Inner Voice Saying?

Above all to thine own self be true.

—William Shakespeare

We all have an inner voice. The trouble is, we all have many voices, and most of them aren't our own. These other voices are a variety of helpful and unhelpful voices we've accumulated down the years from people we've known in our lives, including our parents. We are able to hold an entire debate inside our heads with all these voices. We can end up living our whole life inside our head instead of living for real.

Let's forget about these other voices for now, as they all have one thing in common: they aren't us. There are three questions about our inner voice that we need to answer.

1. What is my inner voice?
2. How can I access it?
3. What do I do with the information it gives me?

Let's get on with answering them.

What Is My Inner Voice?

Your inner voice is the real you, expressing itself. It is the key voice to listen to if you want to find yourself. But, for many of us, it is not an easy voice to hear directly. For one thing, it is usually drowned out by all the other voices that are chattering away in our skull! We need to notice when it's trying to tell us something. Our feelings or intuition will come into play at these times.

Feelings as a Barometer

Let's say we have a big decision to make—do I accept a marriage proposal? Decisions don't come much bigger than that!

Inside your head, a debate thunders away.

Do I? Don't I?

Why not?

Well, you love him or her, don't you?

You've been together for 2 years.

Your family likes them.

What happens if you say no?

And so on.

This is a debate that often involves all the other voices we've accumulated down the years. We can tell these aren't really our voices, through some telltale signs. Firstly, each of these voices will have a distinctive sound, as if they are being uttered by a specific somebody else. They could sound exasperated, funny, worried, whining, optimistic, caring, scolding, or anything else. We can often tell the voice is male or female, and if we analyze each individual voice we can sometimes work out whose voice it is we are *hearing* in our head. Meanwhile, our inner voice whispers, and doesn't get heard directly.

However, while considering the marriage decision, we get a feeling of some kind, good or not good. That's where our inner voice is expressing itself, if only we'd bother to listen to it. So, the way to get at our inner voice is to ask ourselves two questions.

1. If I accept the proposal, how will I feel?
2. If I reject the proposal, how will I feel?

This is how your feelings in the moment will tell you what your inner voice is up to.

Your feelings about things, events, people, places, and decisions will tell you something about what your inner voice wants to say. Listen to your feelings. How many times when you ignored them in the past did you live to regret the fact?

M Scott Peck [1], author of *The road less travelled*, talks of a crossroads decision he made as a child about his school. Attending a prestigious school, he became increasingly disillusioned, even though he was unable to explain why. He simply hated it. When he told his parents eventually that he would not return the following term, he was sent off to see a psychiatrist. By this stage, he was depressed, even considering suicide. It was at this point that he decided to be himself, and saw the psychiatrist, telling him that he would never return to that school again. He accepted psychiatric treatment, a step into the unknown, but taking his destiny into his own hands.

As the above example illustrates, feelings are one barometer to your inner voice. Intuition is another.

Intuition as a Barometer

Intuition, gut feeling, sixth sense, call it what you will. Some people have a stronger sense of intuition than others. But we all have an intuitive sense, which kicks in at times.

- You're walking along the street, and someone is walking toward you. Do you stay on this side of the road?
- You've just met someone for the first time. Do you like them? Do you trust them?
- You have to make a snap decision. Which way do you jump?

If you're like me, you will remember times when you were in situations where your intuition told you something, but you ignored it. What happened? Was your gut reaction proved right in retrospect? I can remember times when I decided to trust someone when something in me advised me not to. My intuitive sense was proved right: they were not to be trusted.

For most of us, our intuition is not often wrong. It is wrong a lot less often than we usually end up being!

As an exercise then, take a situation where your intuition told you something, and answer the following questions.

1. What was the situation?
2. What did your intuition tell you to do?
3. What did you do in practice—follow your intuition, or do something else?
4. What was the outcome of your action?

Intuition is another measure of what your inner voice is telling you. Again, we can choose whether to listen to it or not.

Our two barometers of feelings and intuition are vital signs of our inner voice. However, there are some challenges to accessing the keys to these barometers. So how do we find the keys to access them?

Accessing the Barometer: The Role of Time

Most of us see time as one of our biggest assets, but also a scarce one. We live life increasingly to the maxim that there just isn't enough time. With economic and technological progress, time is becoming scarcer as we cram our days with more and more stuff. Many of us now answer more e-mails in one day than our parents used to write letters in 1 year.

One of the roles served by time in modern society is to effectively silence the inner voice: we just don't have the time to listen to it. Listening to your inner voice is a bit like listening to a child when you're in a rush. Often, we don't stop to listen, because they're hesitant in saying what they are trying to say. Only later in life will we regret not stopping to listen to them.

The role of time in silencing the inner voice was alluded to beautifully by Eckhart Tolle. In a video, available online [2], Tolle talks about the *now*, the present moment we live in. You might recollect his assertion from chapter 2 above, that the 90 percent of the world's population that are considered normal he would classify as insane. It is not sane to live the whole of your life worrying about the past, or focusing on the future, and missing the only bit of your life that actually exists—the present. The future exists only as a thought in your head; it doesn't yet exist in reality. The consequence of our *insane* approach is that the present moment simply becomes a means to an end, to getting to the future we want. However, this approach to living is not recognized as insanity because it is normal (i.e., common) practice, and if it's normal, then it's not classified as an illness.

In *The power of now* [3], Tolle refers extensively to the need to end the delusion of time, and powerfully describes the consequences of our failure to do this. Being on the time treadmill gives us:

> the compulsion to live almost exclusively through memory and anticipation. This creates an endless preoccupation with past and future and an unwillingness to honour and acknowledge the present moment and allow it to be. The compulsion arises because the past gives you an identity and the future offers the promise of salvation, of fulfilment in whatever form. Both are illusions. (Tolle, 1999)

The only antidote to our issue with time is to slow down, and focus more on the present moment. This does present a chicken and egg challenge for us all. On the one hand, until we start to listen to our inner voice, we won't see clearly enough our true self, and that means we must slow down. On the other hand, having our wardrobe of masks means having to continuously prepare for the next interaction: which mask will we wear this time?

Of course, if you slow down, the masks might start falling off. What would happen if you just stopped? It is no coincidence that many people have their best ideas when they go on holiday. This should be no surprise, because one of the first things we do is to remove some of our day-to-day masks, and slow down. That allows our inner voice space to make itself known. As a result, we have all those ideas we never have the rest of the time; write this book, visit that country, make new resolutions, and the like.

I've taken this process to its natural conclusion when it comes to time, and I'm not unique. Many people have to become ill before they make the decision to slow down, and get off the merry-go-round. In my case, it happened as the result of a holiday I took in Peru in 2008. I love learning about ancient civilizations, and even took a walk up the Inca Trail, to see the ancient remains of Machu Picchu. All the while I developed a serious illness that put me in hospital. That moment, and the weeks that followed, not only gave me the mother of all life scares, but it slowed me down enough for my inner voice to emerge, continuing the work my holiday had started.

In the end, my inner voice led me to make some key life decisions, including taking up writing, and becoming self-employed. Slowing down helps you listen to your inner voice, and listening to it allows more of the real you to emerge. It's a simple principle, but that doesn't necessarily make it easy to do.

On the other hand, masking who you truly are makes time all important, and you're more likely to succumb to the insanity of living your entire life worrying about the next scene. Removing the masks allows you to live in the present. As Mark Twain [4] once said, "if you tell the truth, you don't have to remember anything" (Twain, 1935). If you live your truth, the same rule applies, and you can simply enjoy the present moment. This is surely better than acting out a lie.

Accessing the Barometer: Throwing a Coin

Another technique that can prove useful is the idea that, when you have a big decision to make, you should toss a coin. As you throw the coin, say to yourself, heads I take this course, tails I take that one. By the time the coin is about to land, you will know which side you want it to land on. As a tactic for finding out what your inner voice wants, it works pretty well. It may be just another way to let your feelings or intuition out to play, but who cares? If it works, try it, and keep on using it. It has the virtue of taking rationality out of the decision, and rationality usually comes down to which mask you're going to put on.

*

Allowing ourselves to hear our inner voice, we can still choose to ignore it. That is our choice. But in ignoring our inner voice, we acknowledge that we've overridden who we are in this instance. However, when we don't even hear our inner voice, we don't know what we're compromising. We've lost sight of who we really are. Then we end up feeling like we're living someone else's life, and not our own. That's because we *are* living someone else's life. What did we expect when we only listened to someone else's voices? So, whatever you decide to do, make sure you listen to your inner voice. Step 1 to removing the masks is to recognize when we have them on in the first place.

Inner Voice and Outer Voices

Let's say a bit more about the inner voice, and all the other voices we have—I call them our *outer voices*. I believe, from my own personal experience of living and coaching other people, that there are some crucial differences that allow us to tell which voice is the *real me*, the inner voice that truly reflects who we are.

Outer voices essentially originate from other people we've known. They reflect a series of beliefs, mantras, and exhortations we've learned from other people. Most of these outer voices have their origins in the formative years of our life. Parents, teachers, other family members, and major early experiences all taught us lessons. It matters not whether these lessons were intentional and deliberate, or accidental and unintended. It matters only that we learned them. It also matters not whether the lessons were empowering ones or disempowering ones. The empowering voices in our heads may be more helpful than the disempowering ones. But that does not make them the same as our inner voice.

To illustrate this, here are two examples of voices that went on inside the head of John. One disempowering voice told John that it was not OK to show when he was upset. This derived from a childhood lesson that he learned from his family. John admitted to having been traumatized at being sent to school for the first time, and this scene repeated itself for weeks. Then, eventually, his father walked John to school one day, and told him words to the effect of *no more nonsense*. The nonsense ceased. The lesson he learned from this was that it was not acceptable to show bad emotion. As John grew up, he learned to suppress how he felt. The result was that any emotion he felt was either bottled up entirely, or it was leaked through sulking. It was only when this lesson was understood for what it was that John was able to do something about it.

I'm not sure whether John's parents would have realized the impact their actions had, and nor am I sure that any other parent would have done things differently had they been in the same position. But that isn't the point, of course. The lesson John learned from this was his lesson, but the voice left inside his head was not his own voice. In this case, it was a voice echoing a belief that didn't serve him well in his adult life.

On the other hand, one empowering voice he had told him that he should think for himself, and not let other people tell him what to think. This voice was a maternal voice, and was reinforced by another lesson from his father. John's father embodied the ability to be devil's advocate, able to argue the opposite point of view from someone else, without necessarily believing in it. Thus, John learned to look at problems from different angles, and to explore different possibilities. These empowering voices have been useful in John's life. However, these two voices are no more his inner voice than the disempowering voice is.

So how can we tell the difference between our inner voice and the myriad of outer voices we have? The simplest starting point is that our outer voices have a number of characteristics that mark them out as not our own.

1. Outer Voices Have Identities

Most of these voices inside our head have come from other people. It should therefore be no surprise that, when we listen to them, we often literally hear a voice that is identifiable. We may recognize it as our mother or father, or at least be able to say whether it's male or female. Not only this, but we can identify what mood or emotion that voice reflects. So, in John's case, the *it's not OK to express emotion* voice was male and disapproving in tone. The emotion behind the voice could be anything—friendly, hostile, condescending, angry, supportive or baffled, for example.

Our inner voice has no such identity. Indeed, it cannot have one, for it comes from us. Nor does it give its guidance with an emotionally charged tone, unlike all these other *phantom* voices.

2. Outer Voices Often Have Antidotes

I remember a comic I used to read as a child. In it, one of the cartoon strips was called *The Numbskulls*.[1] It depicted a number of small characters inside a child's head that spent all their time arguing about what the child should do in a variety of particular situations. The fun in the cartoon strip came from the fact that they were always arguing!

Of course, in real life, it isn't as much fun. Outer voices spend the time arguing their cases, and it's usually the same case over and over again. A necessary part of that argument is that there will often be a voice in opposition. The debate rages on inside our head while we work out what to do.

3. Outer Voices Talk at Us

Outer voices are often characterized by the fact that they talk to us, sometimes at us, other times down to us. The voice uses the word *you* as in, you should do this, or do that. It talks to us as if we are a separate person, and it is doing the ordering around, issuing of advice, cajoling, berating, or encouraging. We are the subject of what they talk about. This is a surefire way of distinguishing an outer voice. The inner voice, if heard at all, is more likely to use the word, *I.* This should come as no surprise, because it is your voice.

Not only will the outer voice talk about *you*, it will give you the benefit of its wisdom, whether or not you want it! With the inner voice, you have to go looking for it.

4. Outer Voices Are about Damage Limitation

Outer voices are often primarily directed at avoiding failure or rejection, rather than encouraging you to reach for the stars. They generally arise early in life in response to situations where we either had a setback, or gained disapproval from the authority figures in our life. Hence we evolve ways of behaving that are set in time from that point onward, aimed at

---

[1] The Numbskulls, published in the children's comic "The Beano." In my day, it was published in the Beezer!

avoiding failure and rejection. Whether we choose to comply with the rules or rebel against them, we are following a voice inside our head which isn't our inner voice.

5. Outer Voices Have Moral Imperatives

Other outer voices will have a moral imperative, which may or may not come with an emotion attached. When we hear an instruction in our head containing words like *ought* or *should*, that's a dead giveaway it is coming from an outer voice. It doesn't tell us what we want to hear; rather it tells us what we are obliged to do.

6. The Outer Voice Talks Rationally

Particularly in the West, we are born into, and raised with rationality being a highly prized quality. This means that many of these competing voices will couch what they say to you in rational terms. What is it sensible to do just now? What is the rational thing? The outer voice won't say anything about what you want, but rather will come up with a case for doing something else. For example, *the best thing to do here is go by the rules, because. . . .*

The great risk about the rational voice is that it comes highly prized in our world, yet it is often the voice that means we'll never get around to the things that matter to us. Do you recognize this catch phrase, for example?

Now is not the right time.

Have you ever noticed how it never becomes the right time, no matter how much time passes by? I won't start my own business yet, because now is not the right time. I won't get married, or have children, or go on that big holiday, or have the frank conversation with a family member, or whatever—because *now is not the right time.*

This is an easy voice to listen to, but it is also a guarantee that when we get to the end of our life, we will live to regret the things we didn't do.

That voice, and our acquiescence to its instructions, will be one of the main reasons we never did those things.

The Inner Voice

The inner voice has none of these characteristics. It is quiet, and we have to listen to hear it. It may even be a whisper, a bit like a young child who is unsure of his or her surroundings. It may well not have a voice attached to it, male or female. It whispers about *I*, rather than *you*. Nor does it come with moral baggage, approval or disapproval.

Rather, it is the authentic *real me* voice saying what is right for us, without feeling the need to justify it.

It is a voice we need to listen to more often.

Your inner voice is what you would be like if you didn't wear any masks in life to cover up. Your outer voices, by contrast, are simply masks you wear inside your head. If you give them free reign inside your skull, you can be certain your masks will have free reign over your life.

What to Do with My Inner Voice

You can do anything you want once you hear your inner voice. The most important thing is to hear it in the first place, during that cacophony of din that goes on inside your head. Then you can at least take account of it. You may choose to overrule it in some situations, but at least you now know that's what you're doing. The main issue most of us have in the modern era is our lack of awareness that we are even fragmenting in the first place.

Your inner voice is the part of you that is authentic and mask-less. It is also the voice that highlights when you are in denial about some aspect of your life that isn't working for you, while other voices work to keep you in the loop and prevent you from changing. Keeping your inner voice in the debate over your life is a really important step to take.

An Example of Inner Voice Impact

Let's return to Jackie, whom we first talked about in chapter 2. To remind ourselves, Jackie was an outwardly successful individual, who had suffered a depression in the past, and feared that she might be on the slide again. Indeed, she eventually elected for a combination of coaching and therapy. Her outward success comprised a big job, following an upwardly mobile career path, and a large house. However, she didn't really enjoy any of this. The job was a constant source of stress in a demanding environment, where her profession was derided by her work colleagues. Her house had never felt like home, despite the fact that she'd spent a small fortune on giving it a makeover.

It took a while for her to realize that the job and house were her attempt to seek approval from her parents, as these big status symbols were how they judged success. Some of Jackie's outer voices included the following exhortations for how she should live her life:

- Oh, come on, why are you not happy when you're doing so well?
- Stay in a big job, and you'll get a good pension.
- It doesn't matter what you feel, it's what you achieve that matters.
- You want others to think you're successful, don't you?

Jackie's lifestyle may have pleased her parents, but it did not please her. She eventually realized that it suited her better to move back into a smaller flat, which felt more like home to her, and she eventually did this. She enjoyed the sense of closeness in a community that a flat provided compared to the isolation of a house. She also moved to a job that worked better for her, if less prestigious.

True to form, her parents were not all that impressed! However, the results did impress Jackie, who felt a lot happier as a result.

It's time for you to find out where your *inner voice* is.

Exercise: Locating Your Inner Voice

Finding your inner voice is not easy, especially if it has gotten used to not being heard. This exercise is to help you locate your voice, and maybe get a message or two from it about where you are right now.

First, take a look again at the Wheel of life exercise you completed in chapter 6. Review your scores, and decide whether they still look right to you, or if they have changed at all. Make sure to spend a couple of minutes on each life area, rather than skimming around each section superficially. Once you have done this, ask yourself the following question: If I am in denial about any of my key areas, which one would it be?

It may be the one you instinctively avoid wanting to examine.

Having done the preparatory work, now get yourself comfortable, in whatever way suits you. You can be sitting on the floor, lying on a bed, sitting in a chair, or even standing up. It is important, however, not to end up falling asleep!

Now spend 15 to 20 minutes quietly, either in silence, or with music that you find relaxing. If you have a meditation routine, then feel free to use this. If any thoughts do creep in to your head, then allow the thought to move on, rather than analyzing it. We don't want all your outer voices crowding into this exercise. This will allow your inner voice an opportunity to begin making itself heard.

Try to avoid setting an alarm for the end of your allotted time, as this will bring you back into the room with a jolt. But you may need some signal to open your eyes if you have closed them. Hence music may be a good idea, because it will come to an end.

Have something to write on nearby, so you can record any insights you have had. Don't analyze them, just write them down as they occur to you. Now that you have slowed your head down, this may be your inner voice talking to you.

Finally, return to your Wheel of life results again. What does it look like now? Are there any changes that you would make to your scores? If so, make them.

On reflection, which parts of your life are the most masked? Which parts are closest to being the *real you?*

✳

Listening to your inner voice is a really important step to regaining your own personal coherence. It is not enough on its own, as we have seen that this voice has to deal with other much louder voices vying for your attention. Having some quiet time in your life may help your inner voice to make its presence felt. However, the obvious risk is that it will be drowned out again when normal life resumes.

What's more, some of that drowning out will be negative in tone, if we're not careful, with the effect of disempowering us in our daily lives. The cumulative impact of negative voices is to drain us of our own self-belief. With less self-belief, the one thing we can be sure of is that we'll put another mask on to disguise the fact.

How do we deal with this lack of self-belief then? It is to this issue that we turn in the next chapter.

CHAPTER 8

Regaining Self-Belief

No one can make you feel inferior without your consent.

—Eleanor Roosevelt

Regaining and retaining a positive sense of self is crucial to living the life we want, and to being ourselves more often. Yet it is something that many of us don't have. This lack expresses itself in different ways. Some people talk negatively about themselves, or put themselves down. Others focus that negativity on other people, to cover up their own inadequacies. Some avoid taking risks for fear of failure. We may get overly concerned about what other people think, whether it's about what we do or how we look. We are surrounded by an epidemic of self-doubt and lack of confidence.

This is ironic because every child is born self-confident and with a strong sense of self-worthiness. As I write this, my son has just turned 5 years old. He has always had a strong voice of his own. As a two-year old, he had no problem telling us when he was hungry. He didn't think *well maybe they're busy, and I don't matter that much, so I won't ask.* He didn't think *they're bigger than I am, so I'd better toe the line.* He didn't think *I've been a bad boy, so I don't deserve this.* He thought none of these thoughts. Good thing too, otherwise he would never have reached the age of five! He simply thought he was worth it.

Of course, my two-year-old son was helped by not understanding words and phrases, and negative beliefs are simply outer voices that have been put in our heads by other people, intentionally or otherwise. So with no outer voices (or at least not many) to bother him, his inner voice was free to reign confidently.

I hope that, as a father, I won't end up silencing that inner voice of his, and undermine that self-worthiness my son still has—unafraid to voice his opinion. However, too often that silencing of the inner voice is precisely what happens, at least to some degree.

As our parental figures move to quieten our loud child, imbuing us with lessons, so our own loud inner voice is quietened by the accumulation of outer voices, as they issue their instructions to us. This is inevitable to some extent, and may even be desirable. However, the problems come when we learn too many negative lessons about our self-worthiness.

Susan Jeffers [1] talks about our higher self, and contrasts this with our chatterbox. She views the higher self as a center of positive thinking and energy, which we can draw on. However, the chatterbox is the center of our negative thinking and energy. To quote Susan, "the Chatterbox is the part of us that tries to drive us crazy" (Jeffers, 1991). Listening too much to the chatterbox results in a life dominated by fear, and a desire to sit tight, rather than go for what we really wanted to do. Sadly, many of us choose to listen too much to the chatterbox, rather than the *higher self*, which is probably closer to the *real me*.

We see the symptoms of this choice all around us. The epidemic we have now in the Western world of depressive illness, stress, and dietary disorders are one symptom. But even outwardly successful people hide inner pain. We see it in the survey of top business executives that I referred to in chapter 4. As I reported, their biggest working fear is that one day they will be found out. That term *found out* is evocative. It's as if our business executive is like an errant child, and one day soon, they will be found out. In the meantime, they live in fear.

We may lack self-belief across the whole of our lives, which can result in depression. Thankfully, with most of us, it is less serious than this. But lack of self-belief is likely to affect us in at least some aspects of how we live. Challenging our beliefs is therefore an important task: our beliefs about ourselves (am I OK or not?), our beliefs about other people (are they OK or not?), and our beliefs about situations (is it OK or not?)

Let's examine first what it is that drives our negative beliefs.

Failure and Rejection

When we're young, we learn lessons about what works for us, and what is harmful. This is important, because clearly we need to avoid danger if we are to survive. We learn, as a toddler, not to touch the radiator because we will burn ourselves if we do. Biologically important to our survival, we are hardwired from an early age to learn negative lessons quickly. For example, we might as a two-year old have touched that radiator numerous times in the past, and it wasn't on. But we forget that fact the moment we touch it and it is hot, and we do get burned. That one experience offsets all the other ones, and we avoid touching it again.

That's fair enough when it only takes one burn to do ourselves a lot of damage. But that hard wiring also kicks in when the lesson is not life-threatening, or even limb threatening. Negative lessons impact much more on us, period.

The plot thickens in childhood because we are thoroughly dependent on parental figures, whoever they are, for our survival. Hence, we are similarly hardwired to avoid situations that risk our being either seen as failing, or even worse, being rejected by our authority figures. Depending on how our authority figures behave in our early days, and on our own temperament, we evolve strategies that are designed to avoid these two sides of a very undesirable coin, failure and rejection. Of course, we may avoid the failure and rejection, but depending on how strong these fears are, it is hard to retain a sense of self-worthiness. Fear of failure does not generate worthiness. So we learn ways to seek approval from others, or at least ways to cope, and these ways continue into adulthood forming masks of their own. When we're under stress, these masks become even bigger.

Failure and rejection are two things that aren't good for us, so we try to avoid them. In childhood, failure and rejection carried great consequences, as anyone who failed exams will tell us. That sort of failure gets us into trouble with our parents. Rejection is just as awful. Imagine what life would have been like if our parents had rejected us (and for some readers, you may not need to imagine how it felt if it was your reality).

Let's start then by looking at five key drivers that have been identified as strategies that drive our behavior. Then we'll examine the wider issue of our beliefs, and particularly the negative, nasty, and limiting beliefs that undermine our self-worthiness. Most importantly, we will consider what we can do about these self-limiting beliefs. For those of you who are interested in this area, these drivers emanate through the Transactional Analysis movement, and their discovery is originally credited to a clinical psychologist, Taibi Kahler [2].

What Are the Five Key Drivers?

Let's turn first to what the key drivers collectively are, before we look at them individually in more detail:

1. They are strategies we use in our lives to get what we want, and to avoid failure or rejection.
2. They generally operate at an unconscious level. In other words, we are largely unaware that we use these strategies.
3. They can sometimes be helpful behaviors for us. However, at times they can get in our way. So, like most things in life, they have an upside and a downside.
4. They kick in forcibly when we are operating under stress, situations where we're under pressure, or where we fear the possibility of failure or rejection.
5. If we look closely at our own behavior, we will recognize our drivers (and our nearest and dearest will certainly be able to tell us what they are!).

There are generally recognized to be five drivers: be perfect, hurry up, please people, be strong, and try hard. The key characteristics for each of them are outlined below. As you read this, you may recognize some of these traits in yourself.

1. Be Perfect

If a thing is worth doing, it's worth doing right. This driver puts a premium on correctness. If you have a strong *be perfect* driver, then you will be good at dotting the i's and crossing the t's, and you will spot any inaccuracies in this book if you come across them! You will be fantastic at correcting other people. However, you might struggle to cope with tight deadlines, or when you have to rush and cut corners to get things done.

If you have a strong *be perfect* driver, you will probably:

- Worry about getting something, indeed anything, wrong.
- Want to work out every last detail of a task.
- Insist on getting it exactly right when a rough approximation would do.
- Be a well-organized person. In your home, there will be *a place for everything, and everything in its place.*
- Want to check things out for yourself rather than trust others to do it to your high standard.
- Dislike criticism of your efforts from other people, as it would imply that you have failed to achieve perfection.

2. Hurry Up

Get it done, and get it done now! If you have a strong *hurry up* driver, you will emphasize volume of activity, and finishing something quickly, then on to the next thing. *Hurry up* is a great driver at doing lots of things, but it can sometimes be at the cost of inaccuracy. The risk is that you end up taking on too much.

If you have a strong *hurry up* driver, you will probably:

- Be a fast talker, often interrupting others and finishing their sentences.
- Try and do more than time allows, or leave things until the last minute and risk missing deadlines.
- Be good in a crisis.
- Leave people behind, literally and metaphorically. Your mind and mouth will move quickly, and you will walk fast too!
- Emphasize doing at the expense of planning, which you may not be very good at anyway.
- Be prone to mistakes, poor quality, and inattention to detail.

3. Please People

The way to success is to be liked. The please people driver emphasizes getting along with others, and the approval of others is important. Great in social situations, this driver can also mean the person not looking after their own needs properly.

If you have a strong *please people* driver, you will probably:

- Tend to be apologetic, even where you don't need to be.
- Give way to others relatively easily, putting their needs before yours.
- Be seen as a generally likable person who promotes harmony.
- Agree to things, so as to avoid conflict and upsetting other people.
- Struggle with decisions due to over considering other people's opinions.
- Expect other people to read your mind on what you want, without you having to tell them.

4. Be Strong

This driver sets out to disprove the idea that *no man is an island*. A *be strong* driver often goes with an owner who looks strong, someone who can take the world on their shoulders. They do lots of things without grumbling, but are not good at asking for help from others.

If you have a strong *be strong* driver, you will probably:

- Put a lot of pressure on yourself, but appear unflappable to other people.
- Have a strong voice and broad shoulders.
- Take on responsibility and additional burdens without complaint.
- Be self-sufficient in solving problems.
- Avoid asking for any help, even in a crisis when you really need it.
- Put up with things that many other people would find unreasonable.

5. Try Hard

It's not the winning, it's the effort that counts. Try hard people will do just that, try to do things. They are self-motivated, and are great at volunteering for tasks. They enjoy starting things, but they might not finish them off.

If you have a strong *try hard* driver, you will probably:

- Puff and blow a lot, perhaps looking stressed.
- Have at least five things simultaneously on the go.
- Talk a lot, possibly too much.
- Procrastinate with a task, potentially creating last-minute time pressures.
- Be good at hanging in there and making a last effort to get something done.
- Dislike finishing. You will tend to start things and then lose interest.

What Drivers Do I Have?

The most common pattern is for people to have a couple of strong drivers, and one or two weak ones. There is a theory that we pick up one driver from our father figure, and one from our mother, though this will obviously depend on our upbringing.

Any combination of drivers appears possible. The key thing about them is that they kick in most powerfully, and often least productively, when we are under stress.

Hopefully by now, you have some idea of which ones are strongest for you.

Drivers and Beliefs

Our beliefs have a fundamental impact on our effectiveness, and on how we see ourselves. In particular, they influence our positioning on the worthy versus unworthy scale. Beliefs are a double-edged sword. When we are young, our beliefs develop as a result of our life experiences. But in adulthood, the opposite begins to apply. Our beliefs start to condition our subsequent experience in life. Put simply, we get what we look for.

What Are Beliefs?

Beliefs come in two main forms: empowering beliefs and sabotaging (or disempowering) beliefs, with both sets expressing themselves in our outer voices. The former type is useful in helping you get somewhere in life, while the latter usually get in your way. (I guess this will come as no surprise to you!) Both sets of beliefs usually stem from childhood. Beliefs may have been deliberately taught to us, as for example by a religious figure in our lives. Alternatively, they may have developed as a result of learning that was not intended by anyone else. For example, you may have been shouted at when you were young, which taught you that it's best to keep quiet.

There is one thing I really want to emphasize to you about your beliefs, and it might come as a shock to read this. Beliefs are not true or false, but they are simply what we believe. Let me illustrate this by example, taking two people who hold very different beliefs about the same thing:

Person 1: People are basically dishonest, you should never trust them.
Person 2: People are honest and should be given the benefit of the doubt.

Clearly both cannot be true! It's obvious that some people are honest and some are not. However, in this case, both person 1 and person 2 will behave as if their belief is true, and it will clearly affect the way they relate to other people. Person 1 will likely be reserved with other people, and will notice the evidence that backs up their belief. Meanwhile, person 2 is likely to be more open and honest with others, and will notice the evidence to back up their own belief.

Once we have a belief in our head, we tend to go along with what it tells us. This is brilliantly summarized by the 20th-century economist John Kenneth Galbraith [3]. To quote him, "faced with the choice between changing one's mind and proving that there is no need to do so, almost everyone gets busy on the proof" (Galbraith, 1971).

We go around in life gathering evidence to support our beliefs, so we can say they are true. The trouble is we are selective in the evidence we gather. To illustrate this, let's take a trivial example that highlights what we notice. A few years ago, I bought a new car, a dark silver sports car. Now, I'm not plugging the car, but I was pleased with it. What happened? From that point on, I started noticing all the other dark silver sports cars of the same make as mine. I'd never noticed them before, and yet there were so many of them! Before this, I'd noticed the cars that were like my previous one. The lesson is we notice what's important to us, ignoring what is unimportant. Our beliefs are just the same: they matter to us, so we notice what reinforces them.

Given the selective nature of the evidence gathered by our brains, person 1 above will notice evidence that points to people being untrustworthy, while person 2 will gather the trustworthy evidence. In both cases, they will ignore or explain away any evidence that doesn't reinforce their belief. So, if person 1 even notices a kind act going on, their response might be, *what is their ulterior motive?* Person 2, seeing an untrustworthy action, might say *ah well, they didn't mean to do that.*

Where we have a negative belief that sabotages us, it can be difficult to change it. For many it means going to see a coach, or even a therapist. These beliefs can be changed though. The first step to changing them is simply to become aware of them, and to remember that a belief is not true or false, it is simply a belief. It can help, of course, to become more aware of where your beliefs came from. An awareness of your drivers is a key starting point for your belief system. To highlight this point, consider the following beliefs. Can you work out which of the five key drivers lie behind them?

1. You must make sure you're always on the go, looking busy.
2. Go on, give it a try!
3. Keep your feelings to yourself.
4. If you can just get along with everyone else, you'll be alright.
5. I must make sure I am flawless.

Of course, the answers in order are hurry up, try hard, be strong, please people, and be perfect.

However, working out your drivers is not enough to modify your belief system on its own. A plethora of other beliefs will have accumulated from a variety of sources. Consider the following examples, none of them positive self-beliefs.

- I'm not very good at talking to people.
- I'm not a very interesting person.
- Better keep my real thoughts under wraps.

- I should be responsible at all times.
- People are always watching me.
- Taking risks is a bad idea.
- I'm a bad/useless/nasty person really, and so on.

None of these beliefs serve us well in life, and none of them are true. But they have a huge impact on the way we see the world, and how much of our true nature we feel able to reveal to others. They all necessitate the wearing of masks. It's no wonder we feel so drained and tired, carrying all these beliefs and masks around.

Yet contrast the limiting beliefs we carry around with the films we watch on TV and at the cinema. How often do we find ourselves wishing that the lead character would take a chance, and go for the option that we can see would make them happy? We will them to do it, despite a perfectly reasonable, conventional option being available. We know instinctively that to take the plunge is the only way the lead character could ever be happy. Yet, when it comes to the infinitely more important play that is *my life* we do the exact opposite of the lead character most of the time. It's no wonder that so many people (even men) end up misty eyed at the end of such films.

These tears are rarely for the lead character. They are tears for the person shedding them, because their life isn't like that. We instinctively understand the life lessons I referred to at the start of this book, but our belief system often does not allow us to take the chances, open up the opportunities, or live the life we dream of—and watch in films. Maybe this sounds a bit dramatic, but it is what my instinct and experience tells me.

So how can we drop, or surgically remove, the beliefs that don't serve us? Here are some ideas on how to set about doing this. Bear in mind one of the themes in this book. The steps I'm going to set out are simple to follow, but that does not make them easy to follow. Taking action will take some will power. But isn't your life worth it?

Belief Removal Strategy 1: Get Aware!

The first strategy is to become aware of the beliefs you actually hold. The thing about beliefs is that, undetected, they lurk around the recesses of our mind informing the decisions we make and the actions we take. In the case of destructive beliefs, they pollute our decisions and actions. Awareness is the first step to change what goes on inside our heads, as it is in the outside world. As an example of the latter, exposing corruption in high places is likely to reduce it, because corrupt people are now aware they are being watched. It is the same with corrupt beliefs and ideas. By becoming aware of them, you start noticing corrupt beliefs when they come out to play, and so reduce their potential impact.

A few years ago, I coached a client who was outwardly successful. However, he had suffered a loss of self-confidence, his mojo had given out a bit, and he couldn't see where his work (or indeed his life) was headed. During one of our sessions, he talked to me about the voices he had in his head that were talking to him.

Initially, he thought one of them was a more positive voice, while the second voice was negative and scathing. As we explored the nature of these two voices, it became clear that the negative voice was indeed negative and scathing. However, the more positive of the two voices could hardly be described as positive in any meaningful sense of the word. Indeed, it spent its time berating him for failing to stand up to the negative voice! No wonder then that his self-confidence was low.

Real awareness of what is going on in our head is really important, so I'm going to ask you to do this next exercise. You will need something to record your thoughts on.

Exercise: What Do I Believe?

Take some time brainstorming the key positive and limiting beliefs you hold. You may want to look back at your Wheel of life, what you enjoy and don't enjoy, what excites you and what doesn't, where your life is going well and where it isn't. What are the beliefs that underpin each key area of your life?

For each section of your Wheel of life, consider the following questions:

1. What do you believe about yourself?
2. What do you believe about other people, and relationships?

3. What do you believe you should do? Shouldn't do?
4. Which beliefs do you hold that, if surgically removed, would advance or improve your life in this area?
5. To what extent do you deserve an improvement in your life?
6. What does your answer to the last question tell you is lurking around in your belief system that you haven't acknowledged yet?

*

Once you have identified your key limiting beliefs, it can sometimes be therapeutic to speak them out aloud to acknowledge that they are indeed what you believe. Saying them aloud often highlights just how utterly ridiculous your beliefs are. But, until exposed, they govern what you do unchallenged. Once you are aware of them, you can move on to the next steps.

Belief Removal Strategy 2: Get Rid of the Nightmare Scenario!

How many of you spend a significant part of your life worrying about what could go wrong? The truth is most people do. It used to be a biological necessity in ancient days, because something going wrong then probably meant being eaten or killed. Thankfully, this is unlikely to be the case nowadays. Even the chances of losing your home, family, and all your possessions is such a small risk that it can almost be discounted. Yet this basic fear pervades huge swathes of the population, whose every decision is governed by the fear that it could all go wrong.

When you say it out aloud, it sounds ridiculous, doesn't it? Yet this type of fear pervades so much of what goes on. We hear stories of rich people who fear they will somehow lose it all. We hear of those who win the lottery, whose lives are as fear driven after winning as they were before winning. Will I lose all my friends? Will I blow my fortune on silly projects?

Let's face facts. The nightmare scenario almost never pans out. What's more, even where it does, it often proves to be the making of people. Our ability to recover from huge setbacks is great, and we are much more resilient than most of us think we are. Steve Jobs, the late founder of

Apple Computers, dropped out of college. Jeffrey Archer, the novelist, survived bankruptcy and a spell of imprisonment. The Dalai Lama survived the annexation of his country by the Chinese, and Victor Frankl survived the destruction of almost his entire family at the hands of the Nazis. Yet all recovered to lead functional, and at times happier, lives.

If we start to shift beliefs about the nightmare scenario, we would surely be a lot happier. Besides, if you spend your life expecting disaster then it becomes more likely that the outcome won't be so good. Believe something better, and the result is likely to be just that.

The nightmare scenario hardly ever occurs, so the belief that it will is nonsense. So eject it from your system!

Exercise: Remove the Nightmare

Think back to the past, when you faced a decision or crossroads in your life. At this point, you feared a potential nightmare scenario happening. Now answer the following questions.

1. What was the situation you faced?
2. Describe the nightmare scenario you saw. What would have happened, to you and others? Describe in detail exactly what played out in your mind.
3. How did this affect the decision you made and the action you took?
4. What was the result in practice?
5. In hindsight, how likely was the nightmare scenario ever going to be?

In most cases, it never comes close to happening, and even if it does we find ways to recover. But this doesn't stop the nightmare from recurring again in a situation we face now, unless we do something to remove it, or put it in perspective.

Belief Removal Strategy 3: Mind Your S's and U's

Many children are raised with the idea of minding their p's and q's. I'd like to change the letters here, because in terms of beliefs, we should really be minding our s's and u's.

What do I mean by this?

Let's start with S, which stands for a word that doesn't serve us well in our belief system: *should*. The word *should* should be banned! Consider situations where people use the word *should*.

- I should do the right thing here.
- I should be quiet when my elders are speaking.
- I should take this job.

This word is a guaranteed sign that the person is contemplating something they don't have an appetite for, but they feel they ought to do. It means a belief is lurking in the background, and at least one *outer voice* is in play. Now, you might say that this isn't as bad as substituting the word *must*, but I disagree with that assessment. *Must* makes it clear there is a compulsion, as in *I must do the right thing here*. That clarity makes the mask clear. But *should* is a weasel word, less directive, and so we're less likely to notice that a limiting belief is being triggered. Notice the word *should* in future, it means there's a limiting belief about.

U, on the other hand, stands for *you*, and this relates to the debate in our head. When we hear a voice that says *you this* or *you that*, that's a belief planted from someone else giving us an instruction. It is an outer voice. We need to check it out, because that instruction might not be an empowering one. This is even more likely if the sentence begins with *you should*! Becoming aware of when we use those words ourselves when giving others the benefit of our advice is also useful.

Belief Removal Strategy 4: Get positive!

There's no use emptying your negative beliefs out of the container unless you have something positive to put in their place. If all you leave is a vacuum, then something will fill it, and that something will be the same or different negative beliefs. So finding positive things you can believe about yourself, other people, and the world in general are going to be important. What's more, a belief can be anything you want it to be, because (and repeat after me) a belief is neither true nor false, it is simply a belief. So you might as well make sure they are more positive, empowering ones.

I'm going to start here with talents—your own talents. We all have talents, but many of us believe deep down that our talent is unworthy. It often takes other people to see what we're good at. So what is it other people say you're good at? What are you the *go to* person among your family and friends for? What advice do they seek from you? What does your boss say your strengths are? What about your work colleagues? If you don't do this already, start acknowledging to yourself the things other people say you're good at. You are good at them, so why not acknowledge them? Or were you raised with the belief that you should always be modest? That's another belief that might not serve you well.

Having given some thought to what others say about you, I want you now to do some thinking yourself. To help you, I have an exercise for you to work through. As you do this, I want you to enjoy acknowledging that there are some things you are good at. What's more, this exercise will have more than one use, as we shall see.

The exercise should be enjoyable, because it focuses on what you enjoy. What is it that you like to spend your time doing? Don't worry about how often you do them; focus on what it is you enjoy doing when you do it. You can complete the exercise with work in mind, or you can think about your wider life. It really doesn't matter.

Doing What You Enjoy

When you're doing something that you love doing, the following things tend to apply:

1. You find ways to bring these things into your work and life if you possibly can.
2. You would do them purely for the enjoyment.
3. They are often things that you enjoyed doing, even as a child; they emerge early in life for many people.
4. When you do these things, you're in flow and may well lose all track of time. Then, when you do look at your watch, you realize how late it is!

The next exercise is based on Richard Leider's calling cards, which outline the gifts and talents we have that we love to use if we can [4].

Exercise: My Calling Cards

Table 8.1 below describes 52 different calling cards. Many of them will feel like hard work, and won't appeal to you that much. However, some of them will appeal greatly.

Taking this list, identify the top five or six activities you find most interesting. If you could design an ideal day around five or six of these activities, which ones would you choose?

At this stage, don't worry about the categories they are in. You can have any number of interests (or none) in each category. For example, when I did this exercise, the key ones I came up with for me were:

- Seeing the big picture
- Bringing out potential
- Advancing ideas
- Investigating things
- Facilitating change

Table 8.1 List of calling cards

1. *Realistic*	2. *Conventional*	3. *Investigative*
Building things	Doing the numbers	Advancing ideas
Fixing things	Getting things right	Analyzing information
Growing things	Operating things	Investigating things
Making things work	Organizing things	Getting to the heart
Shaping environments	Processing things	of matters
Solving problems	Straightening things up	Putting the pieces together
		Researching things
		Translating things
4. *Enterprising*	5. *Social*	6. *Artistic*
Bringing out potential	Awakening spirit	Adding humor
Empowering others	Bringing joy	Breaking molds
Exploring the way	Building relationships	Creating things
Making deals	Creating dialogue	Composing things
Managing things	Creating trust	Designing things
Opening doors	Facilitating change	Moving through space
Persuading people	Getting participation	Performing events
Selling intangibles	Giving care	Seeing possibilities
Starting things	Healing wounds	Seeing the big picture
	Helping overcome obstacles	Writing things
	Instructing people	
	Resolving disputes	

As you work through this exercise, please add anything else if you identify an interest or passion for yourself which is not represented on this list.

Having completed the above exercise, now list your calling cards in order, starting with the strongest. Are they spread around each of the six categories, or are they concentrated in one or two of them?

✳

There are many uses for this exercise. One obvious use would be to assess the extent that you are being yourself in your life. The interests you have listed will closely resemble the things you would love to do if you could remove all your masks.

However, in relation to beliefs, the main thing to be aware of is that the activities on your list are going to be things you're naturally good at. So acknowledge to yourself the gifts you possess that you can offer other people. It doesn't really matter which ones you have; they all matter in the scheme of things. Give yourself a pat on the back, acknowledge the things you are good at, and keep repeating that acknowledgment until you start really believing it. Why should you not be good at stuff?

Don't just get positive about yourself though, get positive about other people. Challenge your beliefs about others. Do you believe other people are basically good or bad? Trustworthy or not? Altruistic or self-interested? Start noticing the things others do for you that are helpful, positive, and altruistic, and give them the benefit of the doubt if they lapse from the normally high standards you might expect.

It is easier to become more positive yourself if you surround yourself with positive people. Life spent in the company of optimists will serve you well. Positive friends and colleagues will make it easier for you to make changes in your life. Again, to return to Susan Jeffers [5], "there is a lightness about positive people. They have learned not to take themselves so seriously and they are a joy to be around" (Jeffers, 1991).

Belief Removal Strategy 5: Challenge Expertise

We talked earlier in this book about the cult of expertise, which is epidemic in modern society and business. This cult taps into a need many of us have for someone to tell us what to do. It provides reassurance, and if we are honest, it gives us a *hide behind* if things go wrong; *I was only following his or her advice!*

In what is an increasingly complex society, it is too easy to defer to experts. The trouble is that if we defer to them too much, we won't even be sure how expert they actually are. Look at the collapses in the banking system a few years ago, and it is clear that financial services experts weren't as expert as we thought. Trying to get anyone to explain what a hedge fund was proved that so-called experts didn't even know themselves.

Checking which of our beliefs are about experts and expertise can be a useful antidote to the automatic assumption that they are right. Even people who are supposed to look after us, like doctors, are quite capable of getting it wrong. In fact, medical opinion is now veering toward the idea that the most effective health solutions are created between the doctor and his or her patient. They are not simply imposed on the patient by the doctor.

Developing a healthy skepticism of experts is a really important strategy to adopt. Otherwise, you will repeatedly find yourself invited to suspend your own early warning systems in deference to them, and then live to regret it later.

My Expert *Example*

This example illustrates what happens when we defer to experts, and when we swallow the storylines that experts feed us, without question. The story begins in 1991, when I was out to secure a mortgage on my first property. This was at the start of perhaps the most sustained property boom in Western history. In the United Kingdom at that time, endowment mortgages were all the rage.

For those of you unfamiliar with endowment mortgages, the theory was simple. Traditional mortgages worked on the premise that, after 25 years, you pay enough of a repayment each month that your mortgage would automatically be paid off. By contrast, endowment mortgages worked on the premise that you spend 25 years simply paying the interest on the mortgage without paying the mortgage off at all. Instead, you would invest in an endowment policy, with the monthly premium you pay being invested in the stock market. After 25 years, there would be enough in this policy to repay the mortgage. Oh, and you could expect a tidy little nest egg in addition, as by then the endowment policy would be worth more than the mortgage was. For those of you endowed with hindsight, alarm bells will be ringing, along with one obvious question.

What if the endowment policy isn't worth enough to repay the mortgage?

I was reassured by my financial adviser, who did everything he could to appear to be my friend. He reassured me that, over 25 years, the stock market couldn't fail. I also didn't notice the level of commission that would be charged to the endowment policy, so that both my financial adviser and the company whose policy it was could both get their cut. My inner voice of concern was silenced by the reassuring manner of my expert.

It was only at the beginning of the UK endowment policy mis-selling scandal in 2000 that engulfed the mortgage industry that I took some action. Armed with a leaflet from the Financial Authorities, I saw my financial adviser again to find out what it meant. I'm afraid to say that Mark the sheep completely fell for the reassurances second time around! My adviser smiled benignly, suggesting that this was a precautionary notice, and that in reality I had nothing to worry about. It was all a storm in a teacup, and would blow over very shortly.

It didn't.

In 2002, I was informed by the endowment company that my future contributions would have to double if my mortgage was to be paid, only 11 years into a 25-year period. It was at this point that I decided that my experts might not be right. What's more, there were now different experts advising people like me to take out complaints against the companies that sold us these products. Incensed by my endowment contribution doubling, I did just that.

For a further 4 years, I fought an endowment mis-selling case against the company, becoming a bit of an expert myself in the process. Finally, at the end of 2006, I won my case and gained at least some compensation for my troubles.

A happy ending? Maybe. But the bigger point is that I should never have allowed myself to get to this position in the first place. I knew enough to at least ask some awkward questions, hear the expert answers, and make my own mind up. I knew I should have asked what all the jargon meant, using plain English. I knew enough to be aware that my financial adviser would get a good deal out of me buying this policy. But I ignored my concerns when faced with a wall of expertise.

How often do we all do this at certain times in our life? For many of us, we do it far too often.

Belief Removal Strategy 6: Embrace Your Shadow

We all have characteristics and reactions we'd rather not have. We might have concluded for ourselves that we'd rather not be this way, or we might have met with disapproval in childhood. A short temper, doubt for the motives of others, maybe a competitive streak, a desire to get our way, or selfishness. We learned in childhood to keep these things hidden, because we were taught that way. The legacy of this is a pervading sense of shame about parts of who we are. It's sometimes referred to as our shadow side. Most people try to hide it, which is not good news because it involves putting a mask on, and denying an essential part of who we are. What's worse, our shadow usually reacts to this masking by disrupting other aspects of our behavior.

For example, we return to John, who we first met in chapter 7. His early life lesson was that it isn't OK to express emotion, especially pain or anger. He developed a temper as a child, and then learned to suppress it completely. The result was that, as an adult, he would often give off a passive-aggressive stance when he felt hostile toward something or somebody. He would hold back on expressing how he felt emotionally. Unfortunately for him, his body language leaked his feelings, often through the way he looked at other people. This in turn made other's mistrust him, not a good result.

Our shadow is the secret shame we hide from all others, including those we love, and even from ourselves. But hiding it prevents us from being all we could be.

Carol Adrienne [6] describes the shadow we have as the result of our ego's attempts to control the world we live in. In so doing, it sorts out anything that doesn't fit the picture of how to survive and be accepted by other people. She describes how "the shadow begins to build in early childhood, when we hide parts of ourselves that were criticised or ridiculed by our parents" (Adrienne, 1998).

As Gill Edwards [7] points out, how we view our own shadow is likely to impact on how we will see other people. In her view, we project our shadow and start judging other people as being bad or in the wrong. By doing this, we build ourselves up to be in some way good and perfect. We do so because "we fear deep down that we are bad or unworthy or inadequate, and want to redeem ourselves by comparison" (Edwards, 2006). To put it another way, we can then say to ourselves *I may not be perfect, but at least I am better than they are!* We build ourselves up by making comparisons with others. The trouble is this strategy doesn't really work in that at best it gives us a temporary boost. Deep down, self-confidence and esteem remain low.

I want to make another point about our shadow side, and why it's important for us to accept it as part of who we are.

You can only have a shadow if your sun is out.

That means two things. First, your shadow is the downside of the other side of who you are, the sunshine. It is a key part of who you are. Second, the only way you can remove the shadow is to take the sun away. If we do that for a prolonged period, we risk losing our essential strength as a person. Losing the sunshine, we end up sitting in the gloom wondering why it is so dark. This is not a great tactic if what you want is to feel good about life.

To clarify, your shadow is not simply stuff you've done that you're embarrassed or ashamed of. We all have those things (many of us in abundance that we'd rather not let others know about!). I'm not suggesting a mass confessional where we openly admit to everything. Our shadow isn't what we did; it is more to do with who we are. At this stage, we don't need to admit anything to anyone else, but we do need to admit it to ourselves.

Our shadow is there, whether we like it or not. Our choice on the one hand is to ignore it, and let it run amok in an unmanaged way, which is likely to prove destructive to ourselves and other people. On the other hand, we can choose to bring it in from the cold, and use it in a more managed, constructive, authentic manner. The latter approach is more fruitful, but most people sadly elect for the former approach. But with this, our shadow side isn't simply masked. It is completely mummified, and think how much of our precious life energy is tied up doing the mummifying!

Exercise: Bring Out Your Shadow

I have some more questions for you to consider. Make some notes on your thoughts in response to them.

1. Describe some aspects of your shadow side. What is it that you want to keep hidden?
2. What do you not want to write down here?
3. What have you always feared others knowing about you, because they would hate you if they knew?
4. What is the good side behind this shadow? In other words, where is the sunshine?

We will consider your shadow side further when we look at the way we express ourselves later in this book. But, for now, I want you to simply recognize that the *secret you* is a cat that you must start letting out of the bag a bit more often.

*

In this chapter, we have examined in some detail the area of self-belief, and how we can strengthen this for ourselves. This is vital if we are genuinely to engage with others in a less masked way. Removing the sense of shame that we are who we are, we can engage ourselves more fully on the stage of life.

The question is, engage more fully to do what? It is in this direction that we now turn.

CHAPTER 9

What Am I Really about?

Your vision will become clear only when you look into your heart. Who looks outside, dreams. Who looks inside, awakens.

—Carl Jung

You may already have started to connect with this question before now, as you completed the Wheel of life exercise in chapter 6, and the interesting activities exercise in the last chapter. Now we're going to go full throttle on this question. This is a good time to focus on direction because you've already alerted your early warning system in chapter 7 of this book, namely your intuition and feelings. You've also started to take the first steps to ditching the baggage you hold about yourself. If you're now lighter as a result and better connected with yourself, then getting a sense of direction becomes easier.

This is a really crucial step. The consequence of not finding our own life direction is that our days will end up being determined by other people's agendas. We'll spend our days busy, because everyone does nowadays. But we'll probably be busy doing loads of trivial, superficial tasks that won't mean much when we look back at them later in our life. As Gill Edwards [1] points out:

> All too easily, the ego packs our diary with busyness and activities, often in response to the needs and demands and expectations of others. Then our lives are built up from the outside in, instead of from the inside out. We get lost in surface reality. (Edwards, 2006)

What are you really about? This is the perfect opportunity to find out. But first, let me send out a cautionary note.

Visions and Goals

Later on, I'm going to ask you to think about a vision for how you want to live your life. However, too many people in the Western world equate having a vision with having a set of goals. The risk with having goals is that they can often turn into more of an own goal. Having goals can end up becoming counterproductive. Let me explain how this can happen.

When we pursue goals at a frenetic pace, we make activity the all-important thing, and risk losing sight of who we are. I remember a great quote about how we engage in numerous and continuous activities so we don't have to take a look at our lives. That is the risk that continual goal setting presents. We chase goal after goal, rather than taking a step back and surveying what's going on for us.

Goals serve a further function that I believe is counterproductive to finding real contentment. They stop us from focusing on the present moment, and leave us obsessed on how things might be in the future. How often do you hear the following sighs:

- I'll be happy when I've done so and so.
- One more promotion and I'll be happy.
- A big foreign holiday in September and I'll be happy.

These sighs are all about the future. The trouble is the future never arrives, because by the time it does, we've set another goal, or even multiple goals.

Given what I've said about goal obsession, I'm going to focus on visioning. Some people equate vision with goals. However, others will see it as being more connected to purpose, something I spoke about earlier in this book.

What Purpose Really Is

Many people talk of finding their purpose. For me, our purpose in life is clear, if only we could see it. What's more, our purpose is the same! Your purpose and mine is the same. Everyone's purpose is the same. Our purpose is simply to find ourselves, or discover ourselves, and then express who we are.

So our purpose in life is to find and express our unique individuality. Where we differ from each other is in how we go about doing that, and obviously in what our own unique individuality is. That's where the vision comes in; it helps us to find ourselves, and in doing this we maximize our chances of attaining long-term contentment.

Purpose and happiness are like the end of the rainbow. The more we go chasing after them, the faster they run away from us. So one thing I will ask you to do as you develop your vision is to hold it gently, rather than grab it tightly while setting lots of goals to achieve it. That's the one guaranteed recipe for unhappiness, and the sense that we are not fulfilling our purpose. Of course, we won't be, because fulfilling our purpose is not about the *what*, it's more about the *how*.

This is illustrated further by an example of the sort of thing my clients say to me, when they are considering making changes to their work or life. Just about everybody says the one thing they want to do is to *make a difference*. Don't we all? The questions are:

- Who do we want to make a difference to?
- In what way?
- How do we want to do it?

With this proviso, it's time to get your own personal vision sorted: what are you really about? To use the words of Anthony Robbins [2], it's time to create your own "magnificent obsession" or "compelling future" which will help you to generate your own energy and momentum in life (Robbins, 2001).

Key Principles for Developing a Vision

In building your own personal vision, there are some key principles that are worth bearing in mind. I have outlined these below.

Set the Intention

Don't get too bogged down analyzing your vision. Avoid the temptation to spend all your time trying to work out how you are going to do it. Just set the intention about what it is you want to do.

Use Head and Heart

Use your heart to work out what you want to build into your vision. Use your head to work out how to get there, and to help with the planning. Your primary aims should come from the heart.

Focus on What You Want to Create

Above all, a vision should be positive. It's important to focus on what you want to create in your life. Many people make the mistake of focusing on what they want to avoid, or get rid of. As the saying goes, you get what you focus on. Play a golf shot with the bunker in your mind and the one thing you can guarantee is you're going to hit the bunker. In a golfing context, visioning should be focused on the hole. It is no different when working out your own vision. Focus on what you *do* want.

Build Your Vision the Way That Suits You

There is no one best way to do this. You can build a vision by drawing pictures, you can do diagrams, or you can write it out. Try to do something that carries some element of creativity, more than you would normally do. The reason for this is that it's important for a vision to engage with your emotions as well as your rationality. Otherwise, it's just a rather vague action plan.

Focus on the Vision, not the Visionary

This might sound strange, but is really important. A good vision helps you to get yourself out of your own way. By all means focus on what you want to stand for, or what you wish to create in the world. But avoid the temptation to get too introspective, tying yourself up in your own stuff.

Example of Visioning: My Vision—2009

Some of you may be sitting there wondering what exactly it is I'm on about. What do you mean by the above key principles? Why can't I just write a list? All of these are good questions, and I think the only way

I can answer them is by giving you an example of a vision that proved to be really effective in my case. So I will talk about a vision I created in 2009, so you can see what I mean. In giving you this case study, I will cover the following:

1. The background to the vision I created.
2. A description of what was in it, and
3. What happened as a result?

My previous experiences with developing visions were pretty ineffective. However, this one came from the heart, and I followed the above principles closely in developing it. That made all the difference.

Background to the Vision

Ironically, I developed my vision as it was the beginning of a new financial year for the consultancy I worked for at the time. The company expected that all consultants would produce a statement outlining what they wanted to create in the next financial year. It provided an opportunity for me to create something different. What's more, difference was exactly what I wanted!

At this stage, I was in a job where things were not working out as I'd hoped. What's more, I'd had a major life scare 6 months earlier, so I was reevaluating what life was all about. My latest relationship had just collapsed, and I could generally have been described as needing a good night out.

Having been the kind of person who'd always been analytical, I resorted to more creative approaches to describe my future vision. Figure 9.1 represents the vision I came up with.

To describe the picture briefly, and in no particular order, I came up with a vision that included the following:

- A desire to find a relationship that would work for the rest of my life, and to try to have a family.
- I wanted to start writing a personal development book, and to write more as part of my work.

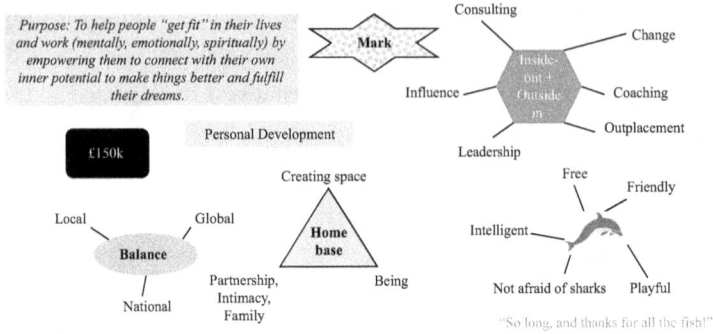

Figure 9.1 Mark's vision 2009

- To do more coaching work, particularly with people who faced career change issues.
- I wanted to strike out more on my own, and take a few risks, rather than remaining as risk averse as I had been in my life decisions up until this point.

In terms of my future in the job, I might as well have drafted my resignation letter at this stage! I even declared a sales target for the year that was less than the company would have expected from me. Professionally and personally, there was no way I could achieve what I'd set out in my vision while staying in this job, and so there was no real surprise when I left my employer within 3 months.

This was the first result arising from what I want to call the power of vision. When you declare your vision with focus, energy, and determination, things just seem to start happening. Synchronicity or whatever it is, something in the universe or the way we see it, shifts in our favor.

As I look back now on the vision I came up with, what happened as a result?

1. I met my now wife within 3 days of the conversation that effectively started my departure from the organization I worked for. Within 15 months we were married, and within 2 years I became a father for the first time.
2. I wrote my first personal development book. This confirmed that I wanted writing to be an ongoing part of my life.

3. I established my own business, something I'd thought about for 10 years beforehand. That enabled me to do more of the types of work that I wanted, including helping people who were in career change situations.

I hope that, without elaborating too much, I've made the point about how powerful creating our own personal vision can be. It isn't enough on its own, but it's a great start.

✳

Just to give you some more ideas before you build your own vision, Figure 9.2 contains another example of a vision, based on what I've seen other people develop over the years. It's worth emphasizing that there is no one correct way to do this. So you should do it in the way that best suits you.

Exercise: Vision On

It's now time for you to work on your own personal vision. I'm not going to prescribe a procedure you have to go through. It isn't a case of fill all the boxes in and, hey presto, there's a vision! It doesn't work like that.

Instead, I'm going to ask you to do it in the way that suits you. It could be at your work desk, or in a candlelit room with soft music on. Your vision could be for the next year, or next 5 years. You could use a flipchart, paper and colored pens, Tablet or PC graphics, or presentation software. You can take newspaper headlines and magazine pictures that

Figure 9.2 Further visioning example

say something to you, and build these into your vision. However you do it, choose an approach that works for you.

Instead of prescribing how to do it, or what questions to answer, I will give you some options you could use, along with some questions designed to shine a light over what you might want to create. If the questions work for you, use them, but leave them if they don't. As you work through your vision, try not to get too caught up in how you will make it happen. Just focus for the moment on what you want.

- Taking the Wheel of life, what do you want to bring about for each segment? What is important to you?
- What do you stand for in your life? What motto do you live by?
- What are your key values?
- What is important to you?
- What big projects or moves do you want to make?
- How do you want to use the interesting activities you highlighted in the last chapter? Where do they fit into your vision?

Bear in mind too, the different components that can make up a vision

1. Your actions: What do you want to do or create?
2. Your values: How do you want to be?
3. Your epitaph: What do you want others to look back on, and remember?
4. Your brand: What do you stand for?
5. Your talents/interests: How do you want to deploy them?

For your vision to be truly comprehensive, you may need to think about all of these areas. Avoid the temptation to focus only on what you want to do, as that guarantees an action plan focused on tasks and activities. Incorporating your values, epitaph, brand, and talents will equally guarantee you a vision that reinforces the principle of removing as many of your masks as you possibly can.

How Do I Know I'm Aligned?

Having a vision is one thing, but how do we know whether we're living in alignment with it? For that matter, how can we know whether the vision we have is even the right one for us? These are important questions, because if we ignore the answer, we may not realize when we're moving out of alignment. So what are the signs that things are going well for us? Here are five signs to look out for in your life. How many of these signs do you see right now, and to what extent?

1. You Look Forward to the Next Day

It's obvious, but you don't go to bed dreading what might happen the next day. You generally look forward to the future. While you might have some bad moments, you will still look forward to the next day more often than not.

2. You Feel at Ease with Yourself

Even if things are tough at the time, you feel at ease in your own skin. You're not putting on an act for others, or bending yourself out of shape. You are being yourself, and generally feeling good about who you are, and what you're up to. Not in some egotistic way of course. But then the irony is that egotists don't feel at ease with themselves. If you're at ease, you don't have to spend all that energy trying to build yourself up, in your own eyes, and in the eyes of others.

3. Everything You've Done Feels Like It's Right

Oh, yes it does feel like this when you're aligned! Even the horrible mishaps, the personal crises, being dumped from a relationship, the bad career decisions, all feel like they led you to the point you're at now. What's more, it's a good point you're at, so these *bad* events seem almost like *good* events, even if you'd never want them to happen in your life again. When you hear people say things like *my whole life has led up to this*, you can be sure that they feel in alignment.

4. You Feel Younger, Fitter, and Healthier

You feel great, and full of life. What's even better is that other people start to tell you how great, fit, and healthy you look. You feel good, you look good, you are full of life, and other people notice this. Think of the person who suddenly blossoms, either because they've found the new love of their life, or because a bad relationship has ended. That's just one example. When you're aligned with who you are, what you want, and who you want to be with, you're full of it. The *it* being energy, smiles, spontaneity, creativity, and fun.

5. You Attract the Right People

When you're aligned, you attract other people who are the same as you: upbeat, positive, and full of energy. In the same way, of course, non-aligned people attract each other too; that's why pessimists tend to sit together. You also find yourself coming into contact with people who give you the right information, direction, and guidance at the right times. When you suddenly find people coincidentally coming into your life, and giving opportunities to do new things, you are pretty well aligned. What's more, the pessimists will tend to disappear from your life, if only because they can't stand you anymore! If you refuse to get off the rails, the train of pessimism cannot get you.

$$*$$

I hope by now you see the importance of a clear vision, as literally setting the direction for the part of the horizon you want to aim for. It doesn't matter whether you actually get there, because once you get moving, you might see something else interesting that leads you to modify your direction. Besides, how you get there is equally important as where you're going. The values, epitaph, brand, and talents are all major contributors to your direction.

In terms of building ourselves in a coherent way, we are now three quarters of the way there. We began by getting connected to our feelings and inner voice as a vital barometer to the *real me*. We then looked at the importance of letting go of things that have happened in our past, and particularly letting go of destructive beliefs that hamper our ability to get anywhere in life. In other words, we ditched the baggage. The third component becomes easier once baggage is ditched, to build a clear vision of what we want to do, and how we want to be.

Now we can move on to the fourth part, which deals with the need to express ourselves. Self-expression is a key to living both authentically and cohesively. The most effective mask many of us have is the one that prevents us from saying what we think, or saying what's true for us. How many of us have buttoned up at work when our boss was in town? How many of us avoid saying things to family, because it might create a scene? How many of us don't say what we want because we think that others might resist? How many of us put a lid on a potentially difficult situation for fear we may not know how to handle it?

Taking off the mask means opening the lips more often, with purpose. In the next chapter, we will look at how we can express ourselves with purpose where we need to, and encourage the same in other people.

CHAPTER 10

How Can I Express Myself Authentically?

Be who you are and say what you feel because those who mind don't matter and those who matter don't mind.

—Dr. Seuss (Theodor Seuss Geisel)

This chapter is about finding out how we can express our true self in a way that gets results. Being able to do this is key to removing the masks from our face, bearing in mind that the more masks we remove, the more human we will become.

The final key to personal coherence is expression, not suppression. We learn too often to keep quiet when we feel we should say something. The childhood lessons are many here; *shut up and keep quiet* is but one of them.

Of course, the danger with taking the lid off is that the pan could erupt all over everyone, scalding them, and you. It's therefore important to express yourself authentically, with purpose, and in a positive way. This chapter sets out how you can do this, as well as giving you some insights into your own preferred ways of influencing other people.

How Do I Influence Other People Currently?

The first thing we'll do is a bit of self-diagnosis to see how you currently influence other people. I'm going to ask you to complete a questionnaire, in Table 10.1 below. Each question comprises a statement setting out how you might influence other people. Rate each statement with a score ranging from 0 to 3.

3 = you do this often.

2 = you do this sometimes.

1 = you do this occasionally.

0 = you'd never do this.

Table 10.1 *Influence questionnaire*

Influencing scenario	Frequency 0–3
1. If someone asks me what I want, I just tell them.	
2. I like to understand why other people think the way they do.	
3. I enjoy the cut and thrust of debating points of view.	
4. I often ask questions to find out what someone else thinks.	
5. I summarize what is being talked about when in meetings, to gauge accurately what's being said.	
6. I put myself in another person's shoes by giving examples from my past that they might appreciate.	
7. I like to give reasons in support of my arguments.	
8. I'm happy to let people know what I'd like to do.	
9. Making requests comes naturally to me.	
10. I make clear what behavior I need from others.	
11. I avoid the need to rush to a quick judgment.	
12. I will talk about my past to help get a point across.	
13. I give strong reasons in support of my recommendations.	
14. I enjoy understanding the world of others.	
15. My arguments tend toward being levelheaded, not emotional.	
16. I'm motivated to use my experience to help others in their journey.	
17. I listen for what someone else needs before sharing anecdotes.	
18. I'm comfortable with getting other people to do things.	
19. I make sure I have enough data to support my view.	
20. I ask lots of questions to understand other people.	
21. I just say what I need, without feeling the need to justify it.	
22. I make sure I structure my viewpoints logically.	
23. When someone is being open with me, I will be open in return.	
24. I share experiences from my past if I think it will help others.	

25. I reflect back the feelings of others on an issue.	
26. I enjoy being open about what I've done.	
27. I can be swayed by other people's rational arguments.	
28. I make demands of other people when I feel justified.	

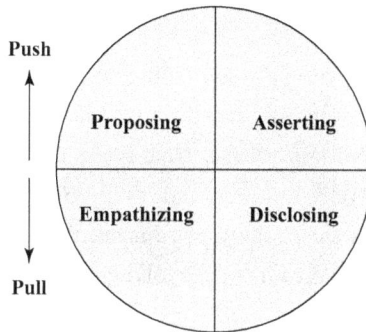

Figure 10.1 The influencing foundation

Before you go on to mark your questionnaire, let me introduce you to an influencing foundation model, in Figure 10.1 above.

Let's examine this model in a bit more detail, focusing primarily on how we express ourselves using each style, when we do it well. It goes without saying that each style can be done very badly!

Once we've done this, we'll return to the questionnaire you've just completed, and give you the chance to do some further self-diagnosis.

Push and Pull

You may have noticed the two words *push* and *pull* on the influencing model. When you're engaged in conversation with someone else, you are doing one of two things at any point in time. You will either be pushing your views, ideas, and agenda onto the other person, or you will be pulling out their views, ideas, and agenda. Hence the terms push and pull.

There are two main push behaviors, called *asserting* and *proposing*, and two main pull behaviors, called *empathizing* and *disclosing*. We will start with the push behaviors.

Asserting

Asserting is an influencing style many people struggle with, and indeed I did for many years. Then, when I tried to be assertive, I did it badly: either ineffectively or aggressively. Many children are brought up on the mantra that *I want doesn't get,* and where we adopt this as a core belief of our own, allowing that outer voice into our head, we will struggle with asserting ourselves.

Asserting is where you have something you want to do, or where you have something you want another person to do for you. Being assertive is not about arguing a rational case (that is the next style, proposing). It is about expressing your gut needs, and it's important to choose language that is appropriate to the strength of your need. For example, in ascending strength, we might use any of the following:

- Could you do this for me, please?
- I'd like you to do this for me.
- I need you to do this for me.
- I want you to do this for me.
- I demand you do this for me.

Of course, it may not be something we want someone else to do. It might be something we want to do ourselves, for example:

- Could I go off this afternoon to do some shopping?
- I'd like to go shopping this afternoon.
- I need to go shopping this afternoon.
- I want to go shopping this afternoon.
- I'm going shopping this afternoon.

It's important that the request we're making is legitimate. It would not be legitimate to make inappropriate or overly frequent demands on other people, which would come across as aggressive. Not many relationships would survive healthily on that basis. But, used where required, asserting is an entirely healthy approach to take.

So how do you match up when asserting?

Proposing

Proposing is the other push behavior, but unlike asserting, it does not come from the gut. Rather, it comes from the head, and is rational in approach. It tends to be the language of business.

When done well, this approach is used when you have a proposal or suggestion to make, and you have data, evidence, or rationality to support it. In using the proposing style, you are open to influence from other people if they have a rational argument that is better than yours.

As with asserting, you choose a level of language appropriate to your thinking. For example:

- Can I suggest that we go ahead with this project?
- I think we should go ahead with this project.
- I propose that we go ahead with this project.
- I recommend that we go ahead with this project.
- I strongly recommend that we go ahead with this project.

When proposing, it is important that you give the key reasons for your suggestion, proposal or recommendation.

- I have three reasons for this, which are. . . .
- My reasons are as follows. . . .

The Mask of Rationality

Proposing as a style is open to abuse, and abuse with a mask. The mask is one that essentially involves dressing up intentions that are assertive in nature with a proposing mask. Classic among them is the business executive who has already made up his or her mind. But instead of simply asserting it, he or she makes a proposal because they want to be seen as more consultative. The trouble with a proposal is that, in classic Western style, it might attract a counterargument. Where do we go then?

So how do you match up when proposing?

Empathizing

When we empathize with another person, we try to put ourselves in their shoes. We understand the world through their eyes, and see things as they see things. It doesn't mean we'll necessarily end up agreeing with them, but we really understand where they're coming from. When we empathize well, the other person will know it too, and so this influence style is fantastic for building trust, and developing deeper, more sustainable relationships.

It follows that empathizing with another person involves really listening to what they say, and asking open-ended questions to find out more. They include the *six honest serving men* questions, after the poem by Rudyard Kipling [1]. The first few lines of this poem are as follows.

"I keep six honest serving-men

They taught me all I knew.

Their names are What and Why and When

And How and Where and Who." (Kipling, 1902)

These questions are asked to find out more about the other person's agenda, not to substitute your own agenda by the back door. Some examples of open-ended questions then would include the following:

- What are you thinking of doing in this situation?
- Why are you thinking about doing it that way?
- When might you start with this?
- How will you go about getting support for your plan?
- Where will you start?
- Who do you think could help you?

You know the questions are empathizing in nature because you can't tell what the questioner thinks about the approach being taken. Instead, they are simply helping the other person to think through their agenda.

Aside from listening and questioning, the other key skill here is summarizing. So, if you had been listening to me talking to you about empathizing rather than reading my words, you might say the following to me:

> So, Mark, what you're saying is that, to empathize well you need to make sure you listen closely to the speaker, and that you ask open questions that begin with words like what or how, who and why. That way you stay on the speaker's agenda rather than straying onto your own. Summarizing here and there would help too. Is that right?

My response then would be to say that's exactly what I mean, and boy would I feel listened to! That is the strength of empathizing. The sad thing is that many relationships, even marriages, get by without any of this. *Get by* is the best that can be achieved, with masks aplenty on all sides, when there is little empathizing.

By way of example, a senior manager called Claire was well known for her dictatorial, abrasive style. But she also struggled to keep abreast of what was going on in her department. People would withhold information about anything going badly for fear of being castigated in public by her short temper. She also struggled to get people to follow her instructions, and more than once she was heard to bemoan this to colleagues, *I've told them once, I've told them twice, I've told them three times, and still they don't hear me.* Perhaps if she had tried to empathize more with her people, she would have found out both what was really going on, and why it was that her staff had difficulty doing what she wanted them to do.

So how do you match up when empathizing?

Disclosing

Disclosing is the hardest influencing style to get the hang of in practice. Until now, if I use a push style (asserting or proposing) I am mainly speaking. If I use a pull style like empathizing, the other person is mainly speaking. But what is disclosing? It looks like I'm mainly speaking, but it is a pull style!

That's exactly right. The key in coming to terms with how to disclose is to realize why you're speaking. You're speaking to help the other person's agenda, not to help your own. That's what makes it a pull style.

Disclosing is where you offer information or experience with the sole intention of being helpful to another person. It might include the sharing of anecdotes or stories from your past. Where you offer relevant information in a genuine way, disclosing builds trust between people. It will often lead to a more sustainable relationship where the other person starts to be more open in disclosing with you.

One of the most influential business leaders of the late 20th and early 21st centuries used disclosure brilliantly. Steve Jobs, the founder of Apple, was regarded as one of the true business leaders of the modern era. But one of his greatest impacts was not on the Apple or IT scene at all.

In 2005, he famously addressed a group of Stanford graduates at their graduation ceremony. He talked to them about his life lessons, and he made the following points:

1. Follow your heart in work, as with all things. If you do what you love, you'll do great work.
2. Don't settle for things that don't make you happy.
3. Trust your instinct. Life's events will make sense in hindsight.
4. Accept setbacks and move on, not losing sight of the bigger dream.
5. Live every day as if it's your last, because one day it will be.
6. Take the things you learn with you, as you will use that learning someday, even if you don't realize it at this moment.

This video has been one of the most widely watched on YouTube in recent years, and even more so since his untimely death. So what was Steve Jobs [2] doing here?

He was sharing the benefit of his life experience and learning, talking about his personal lessons, with the intention of enabling other people to live fuller lives. So rather than issue Ten Commandments telling the graduates what to do, he disclosed key moments from his own life, so that his audience could draw their own conclusions.

This is an example of disclosure at its best.

Self-Diagnosis Questions

Before we move on, it's worth taking a little time to consider how you use each of the four influencing styles. So, taking each of the four styles in turn (Asserting, Proposing, Empathizing, and Disclosing), consider the following questions:

1. To what extent do I use the influencing style in question?' Underuse it? Overuse it?
2. How well do I use it?
3. When was the last time I used this influence style? Who with? How well did it go, both from my viewpoint, and the other person's?

Guidelines for Marking Your Questionnaire

Now that we have covered each of the four influencing styles, let's return to the questionnaire you completed earlier in this chapter. Using Table 10.2 below, add up the total scores for each influencing style.

The results will give you an indication of the frequency with which you tend to resort to the four influencing styles mentioned in this model. Now that you have this, here are some further questions to ask yourself.

1. To what extent do the questionnaire results fit with my own impressions of the influencing styles that I use?
2. Which style do I use most often? Least often?
3. Overall, which style is my strongest? My weakest?
4. Where do I misuse styles? What masks am I wearing when I do this?

✳

Hopefully, you will now recognize the ways in which you try to influence other people. Now we're going to expand the scope of our inquiry again.

Table 10.2 Marking your influence questionnaire

Influencing style	Add up scores from questions . . .	Total score
Asserting	1 + 8 + 9 + 10 + 18 + 21 + 28	
Proposing	3 + 7 + 13 + 15 + 19 + 22 + 27	
Empathizing	2 + 4 + 5 + 11 + 14 + 20 + 25	
Disclosing	6 + 12 + 16 + 17 + 23 + 24 + 26	

To remind ourselves, the key themes we are focused on are self-expression, and the masks we wear that may prevent this.

With some initial diagnosis done on influencing, we can now look at these two remaining questions:

1. How can I express the *real me*? and
2. How can I minimize my need for masks, so that I can live a more authentic, fulfilling life?

I'm now going to cover some key approaches that will empower you to achieve both of the above challenges, while respecting the rights of others to do the same.

Playing to Your Strengths

We talked earlier in the book about our own belief system, which is often based on the idea that we are inadequate or undeserving. This is fortified by the approach many of us face at work, with bosses and companies focusing on our weaknesses. A premium is placed on trying to overcome our weakest links, and to become better at the things we're not good at.

This activity is a near complete waste of time.

Focusing on our weaknesses takes us away from doing something far more productive and enjoyable: maximizing our strengths. Focusing on weakness also fuels our sense that we are unworthy, undermines our self-confidence, and results in our being less than we could be. Often much less.

Sometimes, I laugh when I think about this point. We would never say to a great comic actor that *you know what, you're not very good at serious acting, so we're going to put you in a few serious films until you get better at it!* Nor would we have told Tiger Woods, at the height of his golfing powers, that *your record in getting out of bunkers is one of the poorest among golfing professionals. Get working on it.* If Tiger had done so, his natural strengths may have suffered, and one of those was his terrific record of avoiding bunkers in the first place. Great rock singers aren't asked to sing ballads. You get my point.

To apply this principle to your situation, it's going to be more productive to focus on those influencing styles you are naturally good at. How can you combine your strongest styles to create something truly expressive and potent? How can you refine the ways you use your most frequent influence styles, to develop them further? Focusing on your strong influence styles is likely to be the most effective way to move your vision forward.

Being Authentic, not Manipulative

Some people are able to use all the influence styles well, even if they are stronger at some of them. However, using them well doesn't mean they are using them authentically.

We have a choice. We can use these behaviors authentically, or we can use them manipulatively. When we're authentic, we are shining our light out for all to see, with no mask. We mean what we say, our intention fits what we say it is. When we're manipulative, this isn't true. We are disguising our light, we do have a mask on, we don't mean what we say, and our intention is either deceptive or hidden.

But before we jump on manipulators and give them a kicking (or berate ourselves for doing it), let me say something charitable about manipulation. We all, to some extent, do it. We may not aspire to, but we do manipulate other people at times. Equally, most manipulative acts are not carried out by amoral sociopaths who set out to stuff us. So instead of condemning manipulation, let's look at it in a different light, with some thinking I would like you to consider.

Manipulative influencing is done by people lacking the confidence to be transparent. They fear the reactions of others, and are afraid to remove the mask. They don't feel worthy in their own right to do their thing, so they act the way others do to achieve what they're looking for. They may get their way, but it is not really *their* way, so they won't feel good.

What a sad place, for someone to not be who they are.

What Does Manipulative Behavior Look Like?

Manipulative influencing is when what we say isn't what we mean.

The great thing about this definition is that, when we examine our own behavior, we will generally know when this is the case. We know when we're saying it as it is, or when we're concocting a story. This is different from situations where we don't intend to be manipulative, but other people react thinking we are being so. That might be just because we're not as skilled at influencing as we'd like to be, or think we are. But if we choose to notice our intentions, we will always know when we're intending to manipulate someone. It is that word *intention* that really matters here.

If we want to remove the mask then we need to be transparent when we influence others, so that what we say is what we mean. It's important that we do so skillfully, but we should do so nonetheless.

Let's take each of the influencing styles, and consider how they might be used manipulatively. As we go through them, make a note of the manipulative strategies you use, routinely or occasionally.

Asserting

In some ways, asserting is the least manipulative of the four styles. The risk with this style is that it is less manipulative than it is overbearing if it is used a lot. Come on, we've all met people who are always telling us what they want. Everything is about what we could and should do for them, or about what they want to do themselves. Overbearing people risk coming across as bullies, and will certainly be seen as having a *me* focus. When people throw their weight around, it is unpleasant. But at least we know it's happening, and it is transparent. The other three behaviors, when misused, constitute manipulative influencing, and in extreme cases psychological bullying.

Proposing

The most common way this behavior is used manipulatively is when it is used as an acceptable substitute for asserting. So, instead of saying what I want, I construct an elaborate facade to get you to do what I want, by trying to build a persuasive case for it. This is manipulation because it operates on a deception. Using proposing gives the impression that you may be open to debate on rational grounds, and that good counterarguments might sway your view. But if you're really asserting with a proposing mask on, it will soon become clear that you are not open to influence in this way.

We see this most commonly in the national Parliaments around the world, particularly in the West. In them, some of the finest debaters hone their rational debating skills, and use their most persuasive arguments to try to convince those that disagree. It is the finest Western tradition, from ancient Greece, of thesis-antithesis-synthesis. The idea is that if you consider the pros and cons of a situation, you will eventually forge a better way, utilizing the best of the arguments.

There's only one problem with this approach in Congress or Parliament: it doesn't work! How many MPs or representatives ever change their minds as a result of what they hear? The answer is usually none. The reason is that they have already made up their minds on what they want. It's no wonder that debating chambers around the world are widely seen as a charade, and people are so cynical about politics.

We see similar approaches in business, resulting in the mock consultation I spoke of earlier in this chapter.

If you already know what you want, it's better to say it. It's also better for your self-esteem to come clean and assert yourself instead.

Empathizing

I can already hear you asking how it is we can manipulate through empathizing? I can best answer this question by giving you an example. Let's say I'm sounding you out on your thoughts about what caused the global banking collapse that precipitated the recession of recent years. Most people will have a view on that, as it is an emotive issue, and there's no shortage of people that could be blamed for what happened.

I ask you a few questions, and listen to your answers, until you mention the role of the banking fraternity for the first time. Let's say my view is that the bankers were the main reason for the collapse. What do I do now? If I am being manipulative, I will start asking you questions that push you down the road I want you to go down. Do you think they're overpaid, with all their bonuses? Which banks do you think were the worst culprits? What do you think we should do with them? It soon becomes clear that I am using empathizing to push you down my agenda.

I may be even more blatant about manipulating you, and ask leading questions like *don't you think bankers should be imprisoned for this?*

Alternatively, let's take a different subject. Your partner asks you the golden question for the post-Christmas winter months.

Where do you want to go on holiday next year?

He or she now waits for you to name a few places, until you mention one they are interested in. Then they latch on to it as a place they fancy, ignoring all your previous suggestions. How listened to do you feel right now? You probably don't feel listened to at all, and rightly so.

Empathizing can also be used to find out what other people think, so the information can be used against them at a later date. I've seen that happen a lot in business, but it happens elsewhere too.

The moral of this story is to beware the trap of manipulative empathizing. If good empathizing builds and sustains relationships, then manipulative empathizing is a guaranteed way to undermine and destroy them.

Disclosing

Disclosing as a manipulative tool? Amazingly enough, it can be, and the way it is used subtly betrays the manipulation behind it.

Dawn, who I worked with once, was one of the best psychological bullies I've ever come across. One of her tactics was to sit down and befriend people when she first met them, giving them the impression that *I'm your friend*, and *you can trust me*. She would disclose information about herself, often inappropriate stuff, in the hope that this would draw out disclosures in response. People who didn't play the game were ostracized by her. If they didn't open up and share their deepest secrets, they were in trouble. But she was also good at using anything people did say to her in confidence against them if it suited her to do so.

One example of this was a new arrival to the team, called Mary. Unfortunately for her, she joined the company having just broken up with her partner, who also worked for the company. Dawn managed to find this out, and even more unfortunately for Mary, her now ex-boyfriend was on the Company calendar for the year.

Dawn confided in Mary, using inappropriate disclosure. Lots of references to her overactive love life ensued, and eventually Mary confirmed to Dawn that this man was indeed her ex-partner. But she had no desire to share any more than this, as it was a private matter. Not as far as Dawn was concerned it wasn't. After Mary's alleged snub by not sharing intimate details, Dawn gleefully passed the calendar round the rest of the team, exclaiming *this is Mary's ex-boyfriend*, and *he dumped her*. This pushed Mary even more into her shell, not just with Dawn, but to some degree with the rest of the team.

Dawn was then able to exclaim, *See, she's not part of the team!* The isolation continued, with a couple of honorable exceptions, and Mary eventually moved on when the department restructured. Not only were Dawn's disclosures about herself a case of too much information, but she also disclosed her views of other people at times to their faces. Her motto, often expressed, was *it's better out than in*. Better for her, perhaps, but not for anybody else.

When Dawn finally left the Company, the team held an away day just to get over her! I will always remember the team manager that day for his behavior. All members of the team were invited to prepare a presentation, to be delivered to the rest of the team, to get off their chest anything they wanted to say about Dawn. Her manager arrived with quite a large number of inflated balloons. It transpired that they all had an event written on them, where Dawn had behaved badly. During his presentation, he took the balloons one by one, explained what the incident was, and what Dawn had done to him. Once he'd explained each incident fully, he burst the balloon. By the end, there was quite a pile of rubber on the floor!

Dawn was a brilliant example of manipulative disclosure at its worst. On a milder level, we manipulate through disclosure if we share information in the hope of getting information back from the other person, the variation of *I'll tell you mine if you tell me yours*. That's operating from my agenda, and is push behavior. After all, the appropriate thing to say would be *I'd like to find out more about you, and I'm happy to tell you about me*. In other words, the transparent style to use would be a more assertive style.

Alternatively, we disclose something from our experience in an attempt to change the view of someone else. To give an example, one of my staff is facing a work decision, and I disclose a situation from my past where I faced a similar decision, and I tell them what I did. But I'm not sharing this information to help them make the right decision for themselves. Rather, I'm doing so as a way of letting them know subtly what the *right* decision is. I'm hoping they get the message. This means, of course, that I'm on my own agenda. Using disclosing in this way is clearly manipulative.

Exercise: My Manipulative Strategies

Now we've examined manipulative influencing, here are some more questions for you to think about, and answer for yourself.

1. Which influencing styles do I use manipulatively?
2. How often do I do so, and who with?
3. What are the results of this approach, both short and long term?
4. What would have been the transparent influence style to use instead?

Responding to Situations

The manipulative situations I've just talked about apply when you have the opportunity to influence proactively. However, much of life does not work like that. Instead, we are dealing with other people and what they do, and we are faced on the spot with a decision on whether, and how, to express ourselves.

One great piece of advice I once received was to *respond, not react*. The key to responding is to express yourself in the moment, by saying what is true for you. You don't overengineer what you're going to say, but you say transparently (without a mask) what you think or feel. By responding at the time, you avoid either lingering on the situation, or worrying about it. Then, when you have said what you need to say, the conversation moves on.

In contrast, reacting to a situation goes one of two ways. The first is that we overreact in the moment, the classic Laurence J Peter [3] "speak when you're angry, and you'll make the best speech you'll ever regret" moment (Peter, 1977). The second reaction is we sit on it, and don't say much at first. Instead, we go away and brood about what happened. We build the incident up to have arms and legs, we get more emotional about it—angry, upset, or whatever. We plan what we're going to say back, when we're going to say it, and we play the conversation out in our head. Sometimes, we'll never go back and have the conversation for real. Other times we will, and what happens then?

The answer is that the other person has moved on, while you've brooded to yourself. It is now a much bigger issue than if you'd mentioned it at the time. Rather than get rid of the emotions at that moment, or very soon afterward, you've let it build. The result is a scene, which often resolves nothing.

What's more, by thinking too much about how you're going to broach the issue, you are more likely to adopt an influence style which is deceptive, rather than transparent. With time on your hands, it's more enticing to manipulate, not least because you have more time to think about your *story*.

Responding means acting in the moment, transparently, and managing your emotion. It means talking about your emotion rather than showing it directly, especially with negative emotion. For example, you might say *at this moment, I feel irritated at the way my work has just been criticized*. The other person now knows how I feel. We will talk more about this way of expressing ourselves shortly, when we return to our shadow side.

But in responding, isn't there a risk of overreacting, and saying something I later regret? I'm going to answer this in two parts.

The first is that many overreactions we see are less to do with what has just happened, and more to do with all the other things that have happened in the past, that weren't dealt with properly. Sadly, we see this increasing resentment in many marriages, where wrongs have been done, not addressed at the time, and resentment has built up. Then a small misdemeanor occurs, and bang! A massive argument breaks out, the classic case of the straw that broke the camel's back. We overreact now because we didn't respond appropriately in the past. Expressing ourselves in the moment jettisons the emotional baggage that would otherwise build up.

The second part of my answer is to go to a different type of response from the ones we've talked about so far in this chapter. I refer to the power to disengage, a power most of us fail to use often enough.

The Power to Disengage

The power to disengage means to take yourself out of the immediate situation that's going on right now. Many Americans would call it a *time out*, and that is a really good description. Each American football team is able to take a time out up to six times during a full game. This means getting a short break to regroup the team, decide on tactics, deal with player injuries, and clear heads.

Taking a time out doesn't mean leaving the stadium and going home. The game will start again, with as much fervor as before, and both teams understand this. A time out is a managed process to be used when things aren't going well, or at least where a rethink is necessary.

It is the same with us in those moments where our influence is not working, and where we might lose the plot if we're not careful, and over-react or roll over. So we need time to respond. How do we disengage? Here are some examples of the language we might use:

- We're getting nowhere just now. I suggest we talk about this later.
- I'm going to leave now. I'll be back to talk tomorrow morning.
- This is not the right time for me to discuss this. How would it be if we meet again tomorrow at midday?

Disengaging means being really clear that we will reengage at some point in the near future. It is therefore not the same as avoiding the situation, where we get out and might never return.

What's more, we can choose to disengage using any of the four influencing styles we talked about earlier. Here are some examples to illustrate.

Asserting

"I want to stop this conversation now, and reconvene tomorrow morning."

Proposing

"I propose we adjourn this conversation until we've both had a chance to calm down, and think things through a bit more. How about we reconvene tomorrow?"

Empathizing

"I'm wondering how you're feeling at the moment, and what your view would be if we deferred our conversation until, say, tomorrow?"

Disclosing

"It doesn't feel to me like we're getting anywhere. In the past, when this kind of disagreement has happened, I've often found it helpful to put things off until the morning."

*

The most appropriate style to use will depend on how badly you want to disengage. The more badly you do, the more likely it is you'll need to disengage assertively.

In my experience, situations where we get railroaded into doing something we don't want, that meant our putting a mask on, usually occur because we didn't disengage from the conversation when we should have.

Disengagement and Coherence

Why is it so important to disengage sometimes? The answer becomes clear when we consider the model, outlined in Figure 10.2.

Viewed in this light, it is the critical time period between the disengagement action and the reengagement action that allows us to reintegrate ourselves, to get our shape back. In that way, we have a chance to retain our own personal coherence, rather than being knocked out of shape by events.

The alternative, of course, is that you remain in a hole and continue to dig, or let others dig you deeper into it.

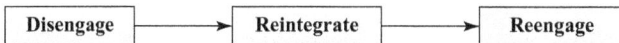

Disengage	→	Reintegrate	→	Reengage

Figure 10.2 Disengagement model

Is Disengagement the Same as Avoidance?

The short answer to this question is no. Let me expand on why this is.

You would choose to disengage from a situation or conversation when you realize that one of the following events is happening:

1. It's going to be counterproductive to stay in the conversation. For example, if you stay in a conversation that has become a forceful argument, things are likely to get worse.
2. You're not sure what to do, and you want to buy time to work it out.
3. You're losing the plot yourself, by becoming overemotional.
4. You suspect that the other person in the conversation is experiencing one of the above, which makes it less likely that a productive outcome will be reached at the present time.

When disengaging from a situation, you should make it clear that you will reengage later, and you might even say when. This is different from avoidance behavior, where you actively avoid reengaging with the person or issue concerned, and sweep things under the carpet. With disengagement, you are acknowledging that now is not the right time to continue the conversation. However, there will be a right time, and when it comes you will continue the conversation.

Disengagement over Time

Disengagement is a viable approach to regaining our shape and reexamining our masks in the moment. We remove ourselves from a situation, regroup, and rejoin the fray at a later date. Disengagement can also be a viable approach over a longer period of time.

You may need to disengage from a relationship, or a job, or even society as a whole as a way to regain your shape. It's no surprise that many people take career breaks, go on world tours, or just do something completely different like work in the third world. People who make a decision to disengage in this way often say things like *I want to go and find myself.* Many of us have lost ourselves in the modern world, and increasingly an extended time out is the only apparently viable option for us to put that right.

It is time for you to consider another couple of questions:

- In which parts of your life might disengagement be an option for you?
- What sort of disengagement would work, and for how long?

The Impact of Disengagement

Disengagement not only gives us the opportunity to reconnect with ourselves before reengaging, but can also affect the quality of a conversation straightaway due to the impact on other people.

I saw this in action several years ago now, in a training course that was being led by another trainer, called Jeff. Jeff was an ex school teacher, familiar with what can happen with rowdy schoolchildren. While this course was an adult one, the difference was not proving to be so big! The delegates did not want to be there, for a variety of largely unexpressed reasons. As Jeff set out the agenda for the 3 days, delegates started to criticize the content. Jeff listened for a while, letting them offload their views (and underlying frustration), before standing up, and responding with "OK, I think I'll stand up and leave the room now, and I suggest you consider going home!"

This intervention from Jeff was a game changer. Suddenly delegates started talking about the real issues. Issues about stress at work. About being forced to come on the course, and their frustration at this. Fears about the organization's future and whether any learning would be relevant. The result was a meaningful conversation that helped delegates to move on, and the rest of the course ran with enthusiastic delegates who gained a lot of learning from the course.

There are many messages from this example. Delegates initially weren't open about their motives, so they were influencing manipulatively. But the main message from this example is the power of even proposing to disengage.

Expressing Our Shadow

We now return to that part of ourselves that we do not like, our shadow side. Carol Adrienne [4] characterized this as our *dark side*, a side that we tend to see as a potentially unpredictable and evil force that could lead us into committing awful acts. However, she sees our dark side as something completely different: "the shadow is more accurately the storehouse of all our unrecognized personal material—including undeveloped talents" (Adrienne, 1998). In other words, we are less of a person, with fewer talents, if we choose to suppress and ignore our shadow side.

Our shadow is the grizzly, grumpy side we often try to keep hidden not only from others, but also from ourselves. It is the *Phantom of the Opera* aspect of our personality. For whatever reason early in our life, it has been put in a box and left there. But, left in the darkness and isolated, its effects will seep into the rest of our personality, infecting what we do. Like a child seeking attention, your shadow side will find ways to emerge and misbehave. On some level, your shadow side will make itself known to others. Given this fact, why not make a choice to try to express it more constructively?

Our shadow side is closely connected to how we feel, so expressing it this way can sometimes be helpful in adding it to the whole of who we are. For example:

- When you don't listen to me, I sometimes feel like running out of the house and never coming back.
- I feel really angry at the way you've dealt with this situation.
- I just don't want to listen to you at the moment.

The thing is, once you've expressed your shadow side in a situation, you defuse its impact. Out in the open, it does much less harm than it does if left unexpressed. But it is important that you do express it in full. For example, say you are angry if that is what you are. Don't say you are slightly irritated. If you do, your shadow side will go elsewhere, and you will end up giving it away through some other route.

In terms of the influencing styles we've talked about, proposing and empathizing are not much use in expressing your shadow side. One is about rationality, the other is about the other person, and your shadow side is about neither. That leaves asserting and disclosing, so consider these approaches that might involve letting our shadow side out.

- Right now, I want to leave you.
- I feel hugely frustrated at how things are. It's gnawing away at me, and I feel like exploding.

Expressing our shadow side has in common with asserting the fact that I am talking about me, in a push style. But it also involves disclosing information about my shadow side. I am disclosing my own feelings rather than necessarily disclosing to help another person. It may help them, or it may not. Either way, I'm choosing to make a disclosure. So, if we wanted to define expressing in a similar way to the other influencing styles, we could describe it as *disclosing about me with the intention to help others understand me*. Expressing is therefore more of a "push" style.

If we do it in an uncontrolled way, we would simply be venting. However, when done well we express ourselves in a less emotional way, and definitely without losing control of our emotions. That is what makes it more acceptable. When we express ourselves, we are literally expressing our shadow side, letting people see *behind the mask*.

Returning to the influencing model in Figure 10.3, we can now add a fifth influencing style to it, a shadow style closely related to asserting and disclosing.

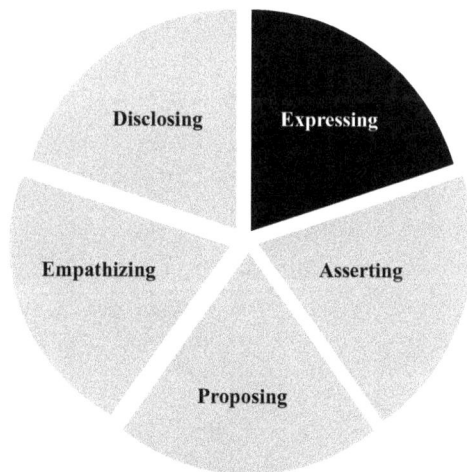

Figure 10.3 Five-style influencing model

✳

The importance of authentic self-expression is central to regaining and retaining our personal coherence. It enables you to emerge from behind the mask, and come out to play. Coming out to play matters. Children know how to express themselves, and they know how to play. As adults, we often find both of these qualities are stunted by what we learn as we grow up. That is no coincidence. The very lessons that stunted our expression also stunted our capacity to play.

There you have it, the four stages to personal coherence. As a reminder, they were connecting to how we feel, letting go of the past, gaining a sense of direction, and expressing ourselves appropriately.

In the final section of this book, we will see how to apply the Cycle of Coherence in a variety of different situations. We will compare and contrast what responses you might give, using the full range of influencing styles. This should help you see what leading a more mask-less existence would look like in a range of different scenarios.

PART 3

Expressing Yourself in Practice

CHAPTER 11

Masked and Unmasked Responses

People say to me, 'You're looking younger', and I do! I feel vitalised because what I'm doing is just exactly who I am.

—Carol Adrienne

In the final section of this book, we will look at some examples of real-life scenarios to illustrate just what an unmasked response looks like, compared to a masked one. The intention is to help you to more readily make the connection with how to remove your masks more often in day-to-day life, using the approaches we've already talked about in this book.

Bear in mind that there are an unlimited number of masked responses that could be made because there are an unlimited range of masks we could wear. For each scenario, we will outline one or two masked options to illustrate what happens.

The unmasked response could vary too. However, there is only one *real me*, so any variation will reflect this.

The Think Say Do Model

To illustrate the examples, I'm going to use a simple model that I've found useful. It helps to analyze how people respond in situations where they are put on the spot, or in situations that they know are going to be challenging for them. The model invites us to answer four questions about what went on for us in that situation.

1. What did you think?
2. How did you feel?
3. What was your aim?
4. What did you say or do?

We can also apply this model to our own circumstances. When answering these questions, it is vital that you are completely honest with yourself. Before we move on, let's say a bit more about each of the four questions.

1. What Did You Think?

As the incident unfolds, thoughts go through your head. These will include thoughts about the situation, and what you might do. What were these thoughts? In all likelihood, some of your thoughts will be voices inside your head, almost always the outer voices we talked about earlier in this book.

2. How Did You Feel?

This is perhaps the most important question to ask. Many people become so engrossed in their thoughts that they don't stop to consider how they feel. Is it a good or a bad feeling? Can you put a label on it? Elated, depressed, OK, angry, upset, happy, put upon, and so on, are all feelings. Try to identify exactly what it is you are feeling, and don't confine yourself to feelings that you might see as *acceptable* to have.

3. What Was Your Aim?

In the situation as it unfolded, what was your goal or objective? Did you have an explicit aim, or was your goal simply to get out of the situation as quickly as possible? Many people will under stress resort to default aims, which are usually determined by either their key drivers (e.g., please people, be perfect, and so on) or by their belief system, which brings us back to those outer voices we talked about in chapter 7.

4. What Did You Say or Do?

In the situation, what action did you actually take? What did you say to the other people in the situation? The power in this question is whether what you did bore any resemblance to your answers to the first three questions. Many of us, when things become stressful, *cop out* in some way. The cop-out, of course, involves the wearing of a cop-out mask.

Let's now apply this model to see how it illustrates masked and unmasked responses in different situations. We'll start with what is a relatively trivial situation.

Scenario 1: The Cup of Tea!

You're dying of thirst. You usually make the tea for everyone else in the room, but you've noticed that other people don't pull their weight the same way. You can barely remember anyone else making a cup of tea for you. In fact, one or two others make their own on occasion without offering you one. As a result, you have decided just to make your own this time.

However, one of the less helpful people now chimes up "could you get me a cup of tea too?" What do you do?

The Cup of Tea: Masked Response—Submissive Niceness

What Did You Think?

What a cheek! You never make me one when you get up. Why should I make you a cup of tea? But then you look busy, and maybe I enjoy making tea more than you. It's only polite that I make you one.

How Did You Feel?

Irritated at being taken for granted, and put down upon. I feel like saying *go make your own tea*!

What Was Your Aim?

In the end, to avoid confrontation. I just wanted a quiet life I suppose.

What Did You Say or Do?

"Can you remind me again; do you take milk?"

The Analysis

Your thinking is in conflict: some of it points to saying something, and some of it doesn't. But the key issue is how you feel. Your actions totally ignore your feelings, conveying none of the irritation that was felt. Avoiding confrontation does not resolve the issue. You have decided to put on a mask of *be nice*, disguising how you really feel.

In the future, you will either continue to suppress your feelings, or one day you will explode and say something you will regret.

The Cup of Tea: Masked Response—Overreaction

What Did You Think?

What a cheek! You never make me one when you get up. Why should I make you a cup? Do you think I just exist to serve you?

How Did You Feel?

Irritated at being taken for granted, and put down upon. I feel like saying *go make your own tea*!

What Was Your Aim?

To stop being a tea servant in future.

What Did You Say or Do?

"Go make your own tea, you never make mine! I'm fed up with being the skivvy round here, and I'm not doing it anymore!"

The Analysis

This is the explosion you may live to regret, for several reasons. The explosion has been directed in public against one individual, but will anyone else feel like making tea ever again? You haven't said how you feel, but you sure have shown it! The person you have attacked will either slouch away embarrassed, or attack you back in return: for example, "how dare you speak to me like that?" Then where does the conversation go?

All in all, you haven't enhanced your reputation for being someone who's in control.

Cup of Tea: Unmasked Response

What Did You Think?

What a cheek! You never make me one when you get up. Why should I make you a cup of tea? You do look busy, but I am too, and I find the time to make tea. I might not mind making tea as much as you, but that's no excuse.

How Did You Feel?

Irritated at being taken for granted, and put down upon. I feel like saying *go make your own tea*!

What Was Your Aim?

I want my colleague to make the tea for me now and again. I want to get rid of the irritation I feel.

What Did You Say or Do?

> "I will make you a cup this time. But I do feel irritated that you and others in here don't take their turn in making the tea. In future, I'd like you all to take your turn a bit more often. Is that OK with you?"

The Analysis

There is a question on how public this exchange should be. If you have an issue with several people in the group, then it is appropriate to say something in public, even if it feels uncomfortable. The key difference in the unmasked response is that you have referred to how you feel. You have also substituted a real aim for a keeping the peace one. In other words, you pursued the goal of what you really wanted rather than rationalize doing nothing. What you really wanted of course was for other people in the room to take their turns making the tea.

Notice also how the influencing model was used here:

"I do feel irritated that you and others in here don't take their turn in making the tea"—Expressing.
"In future, I'd like you all to take your turn a bit more often"—Asserting.

Scenario 2: Unfair Criticism

You are in a weekly team meeting at work, during which the boss goes through everything that has been done; what's gone well, what the problems are, and who is going to do what in the next week. Earlier in the week, he expressed criticism of the way you were handling a project in front of the team. You thought the criticism was unfair, and in any event he should not have said it in a public meeting. You remember going red and feeling uncomfortable at the time. Your boss has never done this to you before. However, he has previously criticized other team members in public, some more than once. You do not want to join their ranks.

Your boss now comes to the project he criticized you on, and seems to be mellower than he was a few days ago. He asks how you think the project is going. What will you say?

Unfair Criticism: Masked Response—Conflict Avoidance

What Did You Think?

How dare you criticize me in public for my work. But you are my manager, and you may have been having an off day. Everyone else seems to accept this behavior, and both Tom and Jane have been carpeted regularly. My manager is in a better mood now, and I don't want to change that.

How Did You Feel?

I feel irritated that my work was criticized in public. Maybe even a little hurt. It didn't make me feel like working harder, that's for sure.

What Was Your Aim?

To get through the meeting without alienating my boss. After all, if he has forgotten the incident the other day, maybe so should I.

What Did You Say or Do?

I made no reference to the criticism the other day, or my feelings about it, hoping he has forgotten about it also. I confined myself to reporting how, in my view, the project was going against its plans. He seemed to concur with what I was saying, so I left it at that.

The Analysis

As with the vast majority of masked responses, your feelings have been totally repressed. Nor do you mention your manager's unacceptable behavior in criticizing you in public. It is arguable that this issue, if it was going to be raised, should have been raised earlier. Instead, the mask of *I'm OK* has been put on.

Unfair Criticism: Masked Response—Deflecting Blame

What Did You Think?

How dare you criticize me in public for my work. I may be the project manager, but I don't do all the work for this project. Everyone else seems to accept this behavior, and both Tom and Jane have been carpeted regularly. My manager is in a better mood now, but I think I ought to say something about what happened.

How Did You Feel?

I feel irritated that my work was criticized in public. Maybe even a little hurt. It didn't make me feel like working harder, that's for sure.

What Was Your Aim?

To mitigate the blame my boss ascribed to me the other day, without alienating him.

What Did You Say or Do?

"I'm wondering why you thought the other day that the project was not going well, as you were rather critical of it at the team meeting."

This led to a discussion about the project, and I made sure I reported how the project, overall, was proceeding to plan. I also hinted that one or two of my project team were not pulling their weight as much as they might. One of the issues that my manager criticized the other day was the responsibility of these two individuals.

The Analysis

This is classic organizational behavior, subservient in the face of the boss, while dropping your staff in it! At least in this case you asked your manager why he was so critical, and there is no harm in showing some empathizing behavior. After all, he may have had a point in his criticism, even if he made it inappropriately. But yet again you made no mention of the impact of his behavior on how you felt. Nor did you challenge whether the behavior was appropriate, at least in your case. In addition, attempting to deflect blame onto others in your team is effectively admitting that your manager's criticisms were valid; it's just that you don't think you were to blame! As project manager, however, you arguably retain responsibility for the result, even if someone else cocked up. Will you go on to tell those two individuals what you think of their performance, or will you hide behind another mask?

Unfair Criticism: Unmasked Response

What Did You Think?

How dare you criticize me in public for my work. You may be my manager, and having an off day, but I don't like this happening to me. Everyone else seems to accept this behavior, but I don't want to join their ranks. If I do nothing, it will probably happen again.

How Did You Feel?

I feel irritated that my work was criticized in public. Maybe even a little hurt. It didn't make me feel like working harder, that's for sure.

What Was Your Aim?

To stop this behavior from happening again by letting him know the impact it had on me. I want him to know how I feel.

What Did You Say or Do?

When my boss asked me about the project, I asked him why the other day he thought it wasn't going well. We had a discussion about that, and then I said:

> "When you said what you said in public, it left me feeling irritated and upset. I didn't leave the meeting motivated to work harder on it. I'd appreciate it if you could let me have any critical comments directly, rather than say them in public. Then we can deal with the issues."

The Analysis

This is definitely an unmasked response! It is better that you expressed this sentiment in a one-to-one meeting, so avoiding your manager losing face in public.

Asking your manager at the start why he thought the project was going badly is a good example of using empathizing. Is there something he sees with the project that you're not seeing? Again though, the key to this approach is that you went on to fully express your feelings. Without condemning the manager's behavior (which would put them on the defensive, or offensive) you have let them know the impact of their behavior on you. Presumably your manager doesn't want you feeling demotivated, so hopefully he will avoid this behavior with you in future. But, whether they do or don't, at least they know how you feel. After this, your comments are a combination of expressing and asserting, which makes your point without adopting a mask.

You have avoided the trap of trying to be over diplomatic, hoping that they *get the drift*. As a tactic, that often fails, as they don't get it!

Scenario 3: Standing Up for Your Principles

You have two children at the local school. In recent weeks, one child mentioned that one of their teachers is a little bit too strict. You have noted this with some concern, but to date you have not expressed your opinion to anyone. However, tonight, you are at a school play, and you get talking to other parents. Two of them mentioned to you the strict approach used by this teacher. In one case their child came home in tears. The other parent wasn't so worried about this teacher being so strict. However, you are not happy with this, as you did not sign up for the *school of strict upbringing* when deciding to have children.

The next afternoon, you are waiting at the school to collect your children, when you bump into the Head Teacher, who you've met a couple of times before. She asks in passing "how are things with you?"

How do you respond?

Standing Up for Your Principles: Masked Response—Sanctimonious

What Did You Think?

Are you going to let her away with not managing her teachers properly? I want this over strict behavior to stop, at least with my children. I was brought up to cuddle rather than chastise, and I want the same experience for my children.

How Did You Feel?

Annoyed and concerned at the situation. Some irritation at the Head Teacher for not knowing about it already, or at least not doing anything about it.

What Was Your Aim?

To get the Head Teacher to sort out this particular teacher, and to stop this behavior.

What Did You Say or Do?

> "Well, no, I'm not alright. For one thing, why is Mr. Smith allowed to get away with being so strict with kids? My Annie is upset with him, and I know from at least two parents that they have the same problem. I do not believe in beating children as the way to discipline. I want this to stop now, or I'll request that Annie be transferred to another class!"

The Analysis

If I were the Head Teacher, I would feel under attack now. As the parent, you have put a sanctimonious mask on, and by so doing have forfeited the chance of there being any meaningful dialogue. Did anyone actually say that Mr. Smith beat children up? Or is he just stricter than you would like? Two other parents have also been brought into the situation, one of whom apparently did not have a problem with the strictness. Finally, is your real issue with Annie, or is it a wider principle about how teachers should teach? The latter point has been lost in this outburst.

Standing Up for Your Principles: Masked Response—Muffled

What Did You Think?

I'd prefer this over strict behavior to stop, at least with my children. I was brought up to cuddle rather than chastise, and I want the same experience for my children. But I like the Head Teacher, and don't want to offend her. Will I put Annie in trouble with Mr. Smith by complaining? I'm sure there must be a reason for this. Maybe I am wrong!

How Did You Feel?

A sinking feeling in my stomach. I don't want a confrontation. But then I'm letting Annie down by not standing up for her. I should protect my children.

What Was Your Aim?

It should have been to resolve my concern about what might be going on in class. But I also had a second aim to get away without having a fight.

What Did You Say or Do?

"Oh, I'm fine. The kids are OK, I think. How are you? That was a good play last night, wasn't it?"

The Analysis

The ultimate copout answer, saying nothing about the issue, or how you feel about it. Note the weasel words *the kids are fine I think*, perhaps hoping the Head Teacher will pick up a slight hint of unhappiness. But they might not get it. Then the parent deflects by asking about the Head Teacher, and offering a comment about the play. The adopted mask is something like *I'm likeable*, and is a really bland mask. An opportunity to lower the mask and talk about the real issue has been missed, making it harder to talk about it the next time. Will things have to reach absolute crisis before someone says something? Then every parent will turn around and say *we all knew something was wrong*!

It's also worth noting the response to the *how did you feel* question, as this is a cop out too. You, as the parent, have answered it in relation to how you would feel about the confrontation, rather than answering the question *how do I feel about what's going on at school*? In other words, you are even masking your own true feelings from yourself, by turning the question into a different one, and giving a politician's answer!

Standing Up for Your Principles: Unmasked Response

What Did You Think?

I don't like what I'm hearing with the strictness, even if nothing overly dreadful is going on. I want to raise this issue, though the school playground might not be the best place. I don't know the full story, but I've heard enough to at least raise a concern.

How Did You Feel?

A bit nervous about mentioning anything to the Head Teacher. But I am concerned about what I'm hearing about this teacher, and I feel a bit annoyed that it hasn't yet been tackled.

What Was Your Aim?

To open up a conversation about the conduct of this teacher, and to stop any behavior that is over strict. Both for my children and others.

What Did You Say or Do?

In the playground:

> "I am concerned about something with the school. Could I come over and talk to you about it tomorrow?"

In the office next day:

> "I have a concern about one of your teachers. I am concerned that Mr. Smith might be too strict. For example (mention what your own daughter said). I'm not looking for a witch hunt here, but I would like the issue enquired into. I don't think I'm the only parent who has noticed. I'm not a parent who believes in rule by fear with my children, and I'm sure you don't either. However, I am concerned at what I've heard, even if there is another side to the story. Have you picked up anything on this before now?"

The Analysis

The mask is much more transparent in this example. As the parent, you have relayed your concern, with suitable respect for the fact that you may only have part of the story. But you have enough of a story to be concerned in the first place, and now you have made the Head Teacher aware of that. As with many of the best examples of letting the mask down, your response here is a combination of disclosure (the concern) with asserting (wanting something done) and empathizing (asking the Head Teacher a question). This maximizes the chances of a genuine conversation taking place.

Scenario 4: Handling the Political Operator

You are working on a project which involves close collaboration with three key people. You had thought you were getting on well. However, it has become clear to you that one of the three people is agreeing with your ideas to your face, but is undermining you behind your back. They are lobbying other people for an alternative solution to the problem you are looking at, and may even be dropping hints about whether you're the right person to lead this project.

One of the other two key people has tipped you off on this, and they seem annoyed at this person's behavior. You now have a meeting with the person in question, to discuss the project. During the meeting, they give no indication that they disagree with what you are saying. They appear to have their mask well and truly on!

What do you do?

Handling the Political Operator: Masked Response—Righteous

What Did You Think?

How dare you say things behind my back, and then another to my face?

How Did You Feel?

Really angry, and somewhat defensive about my role in the project. Who else knows about this stuff going on behind my back?

What Was Your Aim?

To get this political lobbying to stop, and find out what is behind it.

What Did You Say or Do?

> "Why are you lobbying against me behind my back? I've heard you are doing this from other people! I'm livid at what you've done. It's completely unacceptable!"

The Analysis

Faced with this full-frontal assault, the other person will either attack back ("your ideas are rubbish anyway!") or become defensive ("that's not what I said"). Whichever approach is adopted will in some ways make little difference. Whatever they have been doing will be redoubled, as they go all out to undermine you (*It's me or you*).

Your righteous mask has given the other person no chance to explain themselves, and no inclination to consider the possibility that their conduct might have been out of order. If anything, your overreaction will convince them that they were right all along.

Funnily enough, in this outburst, you didn't actually say how you felt—angry and defensive. Instead, you showed it in all its ferocity, and upped the ante by saying you were livid. Is livid the same thing as angry?

Handling the Political Operator: Masked Response—Avoidance

What Did You Think?

I don't like people talking about me behind my back. I'd prefer them to like me. So best to have a chat, and try to win them round, while letting them know diplomatically that I know something. They might get the hint.

How Did You Feel?

Really angry, and somewhat defensive about my role in the project. Who else knows about this stuff going on behind my back?

What Was Your Aim?

To find a way to stop him from going behind my back, without making the situation worse. I'd rather not be in the same room as him.

What Did You Say or Do?

"I know some people would like this project to be managed differently. I'd like to know what your thoughts are on this. I'm sounding everybody out at the moment."

The Analysis

You haven't said directly what you suspect about the other person's conduct. Nor have you said anything about how it makes you feel. If anything, by saying that *some people* would like this project to be managed differently, you have given the impression that they may not be alone in their view, encouraging more hidden dissent. Have you also given a misleading impression by saying that you're sounding everybody out, unless you do indeed plan to?

If they are trying to undermine you, you now look weak and indecisive in their eyes. This is not a good combination.

Handling the Political Operator: Unmasked Response

What Did You Think?

Why are you talking about me behind my back and then saying another thing to my face? I want to know what you're really thinking, then I can better deal with it. I also want to get a better idea on whether you are the only protestor.

How Did You Feel?

Really angry, and somewhat defensive about my role in the project. Who else knows about this stuff going on behind my back?

What Was Your Aim?

To bring out into the open the fact that I know some things have been said, and let them know what I feel about it. I also want to find out what their side of the story is.

What Did You Say or Do?

> "I wanted to talk to you about this project. It seems to me that you may have some areas of disagreement with my approach on this. I must admit I feel annoyed to hear this, given that I haven't heard from you directly. I'd like to find out more about what you think about the project and my role, because clearly we need to work together on this. I also don't want to assume that I've heard a completely accurate picture."

The Analysis

The result of this approach is likely to be a much more open dialogue. You have made it clear how you feel but without rushing to judgment on the conduct of your colleague. Could it all be a misunderstanding? Did the person who told you have their own political agenda? The truth is that, at this stage, you don't know for sure. You have given your colleague the opportunity to put their own side of the story, so if they have a point in their disagreement, you are more likely to hear about it now.

Scenario 5: Performance Failure

One of your staff is not performing to the standard required, and this is being noticed by his colleagues. You suspect there are mitigating circumstances behind this recent decline in performance, as you know something about his domestic circumstances. You actually feel considerable sympathy for the young man. However, the fact remains that he is not performing acceptably. If it continues like this, and you follow procedure, he will soon be out of a job.

You also suspect that telling him this would be just the sort of thing that will tip him over the edge, resulting in the bad ending you are hoping to avoid. So you will need to be careful how you raise this issue.

Performance Failure: Masked Response—Managerial Mask

What Did You Think?

Joe is not performing and the standard needs to improve, full stop. My job is to manage his performance, and right now I'm not doing that. He might have issues outside work, but don't we all? Sometimes you just have to get on with it.

How Did You Feel?

Sad for Joe's circumstances, and concerned about his future. I feel low personally about having to tackle this.

What Was Your Aim?

To get him to see that his performance must improve, and quickly.

What Did You Say or Do?

> "Joe, I need to talk to you about your performance, which is well below expectations. I know there may be outside circumstances, and I feel a bit guilty telling you this, but other people can put these things to one side when they come to work. What's stopping you from doing the same? We are talking about a potential disciplinary situation here if it goes on like this. You might not even survive. So how can we improve things?"

The Analysis

This is a very rational approach. As the manager, you are hiding behind the *I am a manager* mask, rather than removing the mask and having a genuine conversation. The result is stilted and one way, and Joe is hardly encouraged to be open when he can see the exit door opening for him already. In addition, you have been deceptive about your own emotions, by saying that you feel guilty. That potentially is an attempt to hook Joe into sorting the work issue out, to ease your own guilt. It's unlikely to work either, as Joe seems to be in a bad place.

All in all, you have totally blanked your warm feelings for Joe, and blundered in with your manager's mask on. You may indeed be feeling guilty tonight!

Performance Failure: Masked Response—Friendly Face

What Did You Think?

Joe is not performing, and needs to improve. The best way to do that is to talk to him and show him that I'm here to help. So I will find out what's going on outside work, and hope to give him some helpful advice. Once that is sorted, his work performance should improve. Besides, I don't want to be the big bad wolf, the bearer of bad news.

How Did You Feel?

Sad for Joe's circumstances, and concerned about his future. I feel low personally about having to tackle him on this.

What Was Your Aim?

To have a chat to see if I could help him out in his outside work issues. To let him know that I'm here to help.

What Did You Say or Do?

> "Hi Joe. How are you? Sounds like you didn't have a very good week at work last week. What happened? How is the situation at home now?"

The Analysis

This represents a near total abdication of responsibilities. The result could be the end of Joe's job, as a golden opportunity to begin to address his work performance has been fumbled. There are two key things missing in this approach. Firstly, the fact that the underperformance issue has not been mentioned. There is a world of difference between having a bad week and their job being potentially at risk as the direct result of poor performance at work. Joe may not discover this until it's too late. Secondly, as always, there has been a failure to convey any emotional response to the situation. Joe has no idea how you feel about him, and the situation, and therefore no idea just how big an ally you could end up being, even in a difficult situation.

Performance Failure: Unmasked Response

What Did You Think?

Joe is not performing and he needs to improve. Irrespective of my personal feelings on the matter, the organization will not live with this. However, he has worked well in the past, and I want to help him improve if I can. If I am to do this, raising the issue sooner rather than later is more likely to give him a chance to improve, before it's too late.

How Did You Feel?

Sad for Joe's circumstances, and concerned about his future. I feel low personally about having to tackle him on this.

What Was Your Aim?

To get him to acknowledge that his performance needs to improve, and offer what support I can (both moral and practical) to help him make the improvement.

What Did You Say or Do?

"Joe. I need to talk to you about your work performance in recent weeks. I suspect you know that it's not at the standard it needs to be, and it needs to improve. I am concerned to safeguard your future in whatever ways I can, and to tell you the truth, I haven't been looking forward to this conversation. I want to be on your side, so I need to know what your ideas are on how we can improve things."

The Analysis

Once again, the mask-less approach involves a combination of assertive and disclosing behaviors. You have let Joe know you're on his side, and given him an idea of how you feel. But you have also let him know that the current situation is not acceptable. You then moved on to engage him, asking what ideas he has at the moment to improve things.

Removing the mask does not make the conversation easy. However, it does make the conversation authentic. Doing this maximizes the chances that the subsequent conversation will move into a collaborative, problem-solving mode.

Some Comments on the Case Studies

The first two questions in each case study are important. The first question *what did you think?* showed a variety of thinking around the same case study. But often, we think we're thinking when what we're really doing is rationalizing. Thinking and rationalizing are two different things. Thinking is important, and what we think about will determine what we then focus on, as we saw in the case study responses. However, beware the *thinking* that goes on inside our heads. How much of it is real thinking, and how much is just the repetitive drone of all those voices in our heads, representing what has been put there by other people? This thinking does not represent the *real me*. Instead, it consists of trapped voices of other people's conversations that we have adopted as our own. This is not meaningful thinking.

However, the answers to the second question *how did you feel?* show far more consistency of response. The only thing that changes this answer is if we're not aware of how we feel, or try to suppress and deflect feelings. But if we connect to ourselves properly, we will be much more aware of how we feel. It is this that enables us to tap in to the *real me*. Then, by bringing our feelings out into conversation, we can have authentic, mask-less interactions with the other people in our life.

The single biggest key to removing the masks is therefore to give recognition to our feelings about the situation. We then need to disclose those feelings to other people, in an appropriate way. Disclosing and expressing are the key behaviors to do this, depending on whether our shadow side is called into play.

Using the influence model means utilizing all five behaviors. However, given the above comments about rationalizing, it is likely that the least useful influencing style is going to be proposing (which is the rational style). The other four are far more important. This might be a surprise given the high emphasis that is placed on adult conversations being rational in nature. However, it is the rational approach of Western life that created the crisis around the *real me* in the first place! There is a role for persuading, but not in its overuse in much of business or society, where many agendas are routinely disguised behind a rational, persuasive mask.

Without exception in the above case studies, using a mask-less approach means a much greater chance of establishing a constructive dialogue, with empathizing behaviors brought in to help. What's more, when you role model what it is to remove the masks, you encourage other people you're engaged with to do the same.

It was Marianne Williamson's [1] famous quote that emphasized how many people are afraid of their own brilliance. She said "as we let our own light shine, we unconsciously give other people permission to do the same" (Williamson, 1992). Removing our masks as much as possible is the key means to making sure our own light does indeed shine brightly, and illuminates the lives of all around us.

*

We now move to the penultimate chapter of this book, where we explore the four stages of the Coherence Cycle as a whole, putting them all together—and in the process helping you to pull yourself together.

CHAPTER 12

The Coherence Cycle

We have to dare to be ourselves, however frightening or strange that self may prove to be.

—May Sarton

Figure 12.1 summarizes the coherence cycle in its full glory.

By repeating this cycle, we can ensure that we move toward personal coherence. It may not stop us from having to play roles or hide behind masks at times. However, it will ensure that, when we do, it is the result of conscious choice rather than a default response to the situation we are in. We will realize that we're making the choice. Making the choice conscious is key to ensuring that the *real me* is somewhere near to the center stage of our life.

To help you use the coherence cycle, I have provided a checklist of questions that will help you to deal with each of the four stages. You can

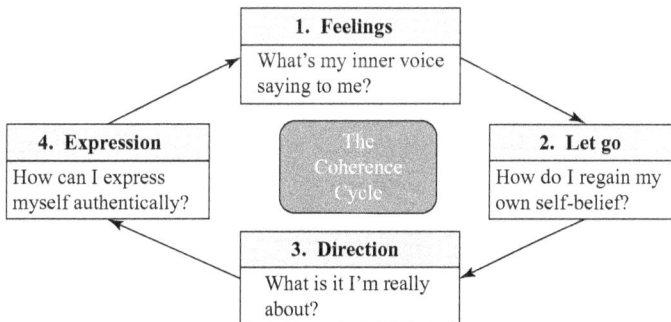

Figure 12.1 The coherence cycle

use this checklist to help you work out what to do in situations where you suspect that you have a mask on, or are under pressure to put one on. They could even be similar situations to the scenarios referred to in the last chapter. While you may not be able to answer every question for every situation, asking them and answering those you can will help to highlight what's really going on for you. More importantly, you will be able to work out what to do about the situation now.

1. Feelings: What's My Inner Voice Saying to Me?

- How do I feel right now about this situation?
- What does my instinct tell me?
- What is my whispering voice saying to me, if I can hear it?
- How happy am I with the different parts of my Wheel of life?
- To what extent am I living in the present right now? (as opposed to being preoccupied with the past or future).
- When can I find some quiet time?
- Where does my focus go when I slow down a bit?
- What is my *I* voice saying right now?
- If I tossed a coin on a key decision, what side would I want the coin to land on?

2. Let Go: How Do I Regain My Own Self-Belief?

- How safe have I been playing this situation until now?
- What limiting lesson did I learn in childhood about this?
- What mask do I end up putting on as a result? Describe the mask, and give it a name.
- Which of my key drivers are affecting me in this situation? (be perfect, hurry up, be strong, try hard, and please people).
- What is it that I believe about myself? Other people? Consider both positive and limiting beliefs.
- What could I achieve if I didn't hold these beliefs?
- What nightmare scenario could I let go of here?
- What *should* and *you* beliefs could I weed out?
- What talents do I possess that could help in this situation?

- What talents do other people recognize in me that could help?
- What would I actually enjoy doing here?
- What is it I fear other people knowing about me?
- What part of my shadow side am I hiding?
- What is the good (sunshine) side of this shadow?
- What risk, if it worked, would move me forward?

3. Direction: What Is It I'm Really about?

- How do I want to live my life? What is my whole life vision?
- In what way is this situation preventing me from doing that?
- To what extent does my heart buy into this vision? (emotional engagement)
- To what extent does my head buy into this vision? (thinking engagement)
- Considering my Wheel of life, where do my natural focus, energy, and determination point me?
- Which parts of my life are most important to me?
- What do I stand for?
- Which key values of mine are being challenged in this situation?
- What do I want my epitaph, or eulogy, to be?
- What is my personal motto that I try to live life by?
- Which of my masks do I now need to remove?
- How much do I look forward to sorting this situation out?
- How do I feel right now about my not dealing with it?
- Who are the positive people in my life and how might they help?

4. Expression: How Can I Express Myself Authentically?

- Is my natural tendency more to *push* (asserting, proposing) or *pull* (empathizing, disclosing) when influencing others?
- Which influencing styles do I use most?
- Which styles do I tend to avoid using?
- What steps can I take to use them more?
- To what extent do I play to my strengths in life, rather than focusing on weaknesses?

- What am I resolving to do now with this situation I'm facing?
- Which influencing behaviors will help me most with this issue?
- How can I use my strongest influence styles to help me in the parts of my life where I am dissatisfied?
- How can I minimize my manipulative behavior, and maximize the number of times where what I say is what I mean?
- Where can I respond more effectively to situations, by saying what is true for me?
- What am I festering about at the moment?
- How will I deal with it?
- To what extent would disengaging or taking a time out help here?
- What does my full "Phantom of the Opera" shadow side look like?
- What are the qualities of my shadow side?
- How and where can I express it in the situation I face now?

*

This checklist can also serve as a refresher on the book content under each of these four key headings. However, it is not a shortcut for reading the book!

CHAPTER 13

Toward a Coherent Future

Every time you open your wardrobe, you look at your clothes and you wonder what you are going to wear. What you are really saying is, who am I going to be today?

—Fay Weldon

In today's world, we face the biggest challenge we've ever faced in maintaining our own personal cohesion. The impact of our upbringing in its widest sense is that we're often encouraged to feel bad about ourselves, guilty about the past, and fearful of the future. The result of this is that we settle for mediocrity. Mediocrity dressed up as progress and achievement, because that is what our society expects us to talk about. We are encouraged to have a personal brand, talk ourselves up, and even watch reality TV programs where we laugh at people making claims about their own talent. We may laugh, but behind their apparent self-confidence, they are often as desperately insecure as many of the rest of us feel. It's no wonder that, as highlighted elsewhere, even outwardly successful people live much of their life in perpetual fear of being *found out*.

We fear being unmasked, and shown up for who we really are. What a shame! If we can learn that, not only is it OK, but positively desirable to unmask ourselves more often, we will be well on the way to a happier, more secure life. Secure in the knowledge that we can be who we really are, and it will be alright. How much of our precious energy could we then release to devote to the things that really matter? Again, to quote the words of Gill Edwards [1]:

> Becoming authentic often means letting go of the life you have known. Your deep-self whispers to you to dream the impossible dream. It often asks you to break the rules, to do the unexpected—even the unthinkable. It pays no attention to the norms and inhibitions of society, family or religion. The deep self is a non-conformist. (Edwards, 2006)

One of the most inspiring people I've ever known was an old man, who was in his 76th year when I first met him. Luckily, he survived to reach 96. He was one of the most unassuming, modest people I've ever met, and many people who did meet him would not have known his story.

His life, which I discovered bit by bit (due to his self-modesty) was a litany of trial and tribulation on the face of it. Born in Northern Ireland, his mother divorced and brought him to Glasgow. Placed eventually in an orphanage, and now a teenager, he ran away to Canada. He then joined the British army in time to be placed in India and Nepal, where he saw Gandhi in prison turning the salt grinder. He also saw time in Berlin in the mid-1930s; indeed, he saw Jesse Owen win four gold medals, with Hitler storming out of the Olympic Stadium in disgust. In 1944, he was in the British Regiment that flew in behind enemy lines on D day, and was the only survivor from his glider. He saw action all the way to Berlin for a second time, where he met the Russian army, and by his own testimony surviving the war more through luck than judgment! He returned to the United Kingdom, so hard up that he used his red beret as a cycle saddle. He saw his days out as a lorry driver, with many amusing stories about things that happened. He joined his mother in getting divorced, and saw much time home alone in his old age, with a dog for company.

This man spent much of his life on the run, with many adverse circumstances beyond his control (though not all). He saw many global events, and I joked to him that he must have been in Dallas during 1963, for the visit of John F. Kennedy. He did his own thing, choosing not to mix very much. Most of all, however, he was always himself, and not someone else. Most significantly, near the end of his life, he didn't express any regrets.

Don't waste your time, energy, and identity trying to live someone else's life. Use it instead to be the best you that you can be. With the approaches and techniques you've read about, you can shift and shape your life. Then how will you feel?

As Soren Keirkegaard [2] highlighted many years ago, our purpose often comes down "to be that self which one truly is" (Rogers, 1961). This hasn't changed with modernity. We are all ultimately looking for ourselves. Good luck, and enjoy the journey!

APPENDIX

Key Terms Defined

By way of summary, the following definitions are listed for key terms adopted in this book.

Fragmentation—The act of putting masks on for different situations we face in life. Excessive levels of fragmentation can result in personal incoherence.

Personal coherence—Our own sense of who we really are, based around the *real me*.

Personal incoherence—The effect on our identity of excessive mask wearing, when we lose sight of the *real me*.

Personal identity—Our own sense of identity, based around who we believe ourselves to be. Identity can be coherent or incoherent. In other words, it can take account of the *real me*, or remain in ignorance of it.

The real me—What we would really be like if we could behave naturally all the time.

References

Introduction

Hanlon, P., Carlisle, S., Hannah, M., and Lyon, A. (2012). *The future public health*. Maidenhead. Open University Press. A summary of the arguments on modern diseases and the breakdown of current medical models can also be found on www.afternow.co.uk

Frankl, V. E. (2006). *Man's search for meaning*. Boston. Beacon Press

Descartes, R., Cottingham, J., Stoothoff, R., and Murdoch, D. (1984). *The philosophical writings of Descartes: Vol. II*. Cambridge. Cambridge University Press. p17

Coelho, P. (2006). *The alchemist*. London. Harper Collins

Chapter 1: Coherent Death, Incoherent Life

Richardleider.com. (2016). *Unlock the power of purpose* [online]. Available at http://www.richardleider.com/ [Accessed 20 November 2016]

Ware, B. (2012). *The top five regrets of the dying*. London. Hay House. p37

Robbins, A. (2001). *Awaken the giant within*. London. Simon & Schuster Ltd. p413

Chapter 2: Fragmentation and Masks

Tolle, E. (2005). *The power of now*. London. Hodder & Stoughton

Stephenson, G. R. (1967). Cultural acquisition of a specific learned response among rhesus monkeys. In: Starek, D., Schneider, R., and Kuhn, H. J. (eds.). *Progress in primatology*. Stuttgart. Fischer. pp279–288

Chapter 3: Three Sources of Fragmentation

Berne, E. (1964). *Games people play*. New York. Grove Press

Robinson, K. (2006). *Do schools kill creativity?* [video]. Available at https://www.ted.com/talks/ken_robinson_says_schools_kill_creativity [Accessed 20 November 2016]

Nobelprize.org. (2012). *The Nobel Prize in physiology or medicine 2012* [online]. Available at https://www.nobelprize.org/nobel_prizes/medicine/laureates/2012/gurdon-photo.html [Accessed 20 November 2016]

Williamson, M. (1992). *A return to love*. New York. Harper Collins

Dilbert.com. (2016). *Dilbert by Scott Adams.* [online]. Available at http://www.dilbert.com/ [Accessed 20 November 2016]

Robbins, H., and Finley, M. (2000). *The NEW why teams don't work.* Oakland. Berrett-Koehler Publishers. p184

Orwell, G. (1949). *Nineteen eighty-four.* New York. Harcourt, Brace & Co.

Chapter 4: The Consequences of Fragmentation

Laing, R. D. (1990). *The divided self.* London. Penguin. p12. It was previously published by Pelican in 1965

Jung, C. (1971). *Psychological types.* Princeton. Princeton University Press

Clance, P., and Imes, S. (1978). *The impostor phenomenon among high achieving women: Dynamics and therapeutic intervention,* Psychotherapy Theory, Research and Practice. 15(3). pp241–247. There have since been many other studies into this topic

Chapter 5: Some Responses to Fragmentation

Marx, K. (1970). *A contribution to the critique of Hegel's philosophy of right.* Cambridge. Cambridge University Press. First published 1843. The original quote was more convoluted than the misquote is, though it effectively meant the same thing

Burkeman, O. (2012). *The antidote.* Edinburgh. Canongate Books Ltd. p9

Byrne, R. (2006). *The secret.* New York. Atria Books

Rogers, C. R. (1961). *On becoming a person: A therapist's view of psychotherapy.* Boston. Houghton Mifflin Company. pp167–176

Chapter 7: What Is My Inner Voice Saying?

Peck, M. S. (2006). *The road less travelled.* London. Arrow Books. pp124–125

Tolle, E. (2007). *Awakening in the now: Public lecture* [video]. Available at https://www.youtube.com/watch?v=fwr4zCuEmw0 [Accessed 22 November 2016]

Tolle, E. (1999). *The power of now.* London. Hodder & Stoughton. p40

Paine, A. B. (ed). (1935). *Mark Twain's notebook.* New York. Harper Collins. p240

Chapter 8: Regaining Self-Belief

Jeffers, S. (1991). *Feel the fear and do it anyway.* London. Vermilion. p192

Stewart, I., and Joines, V. (1987). *TA Today—A new introduction to transactional analysis.* Nottingham & Chapel Hill. Lifespace Publishing. pp155–164

Galbraith, J. K. (1971). *A contemporary guide to economics, peace and laughter*. London. Andre Deutsch Ltd. p50

Leider, R. J. and Shapiro, D. A. (2015). *Work reimagined: Uncover your calling*. Oakland. Berrett-Koehler Publishers

Jeffers, S. (1991). *Feel the fear and do it anyway*. London. Vermilion. p92

Adrienne, C. (1998). *The purpose of your life*. London. Thorsons. p217

Edwards, G. (2006). *Wild love*. London. Piatkus Books. p106

Chapter 9: What Am I Really about?

Edwards, G. (2006). *Wild love*. London. Piatkus Books. p138

Robbins, A. (2001). *Awaken the giant within*. London. Simon & Schuster Ltd. pp271–308

Chapter 10: How Can I Express Myself Authentically?

Kipling, R. (1902). *Just so stories for little children*. New York. Doubleday, Page & Co. p83

Jobs, S. (2005). *Commencement address to Stanford University*. [video]. Available at https://www.youtube.com/watch?v=UF8uR6Z6KLc [Accessed 24 November 2016]

Peter, L. J. (1977). *Quotations for our time*. London. MacDonald & Co (Publisher's) Ltd. p51

Adrienne, C. (1998). *The purpose of your life*. London. Thorsons. p217

Chapter 11: Masked and Unmasked Responses

Williamson, M. (1992). *A return to love*. New York. Harper Collins. pp190–191

Chapter 13: Toward a Coherent Future

Edwards, G. (2006). *Wild love*. London. Piatkus Books. p14

Rogers, C. R. (1961). *On becoming a person: A therapist's view of psychotherapy*. Boston. Houghton Mifflin Company. p166. The original reference for the quotation is; Kierkegaard, S. (1849). *Sygdommen til Døden: En christelig psychologisk Udvikling til Opbyggelse og Opvækkelse*. Kopenhagen. Reitzels.

Index

OTHER TITLES IN THE HUMAN RESOURCE MANAGEMENT AND ORGANIZATIONAL BEHAVIOR COLLECTION

- *The Illusion of Inclusion: Global Inclusion, Unconscious Bias, and the Bottom Line* by Helen Turnbull
- *On All Cylinders: The Entrepreneur's Handbook* by Ron Robinson
- *The Resilience Advantage: Stop Managing Stress and Find Your Resilience* by Richard S. Citrin and Alan Weiss
- *Successful Interviewing: A Talent-Focused Approach to Successful Recruitment and Selection* by Tony Miller
- *HR Analytics and Innovations in Workforce Planning* by Tony Miller
- *Success: Theory and Practice* by Michael Edmondson
- *Leading The Positive Organization: Actions, Tools, and Processes* by Thomas N. Duening, Donald G. Gardner, Dustin Bluhm, Andrew J. Czaplewski, and Thomas Martin Key
- *Performance Leadership* by Karen Moustafa Leonard and Fatma Pakdil
- *The New Leader: Harnessing The Power of Creativity to Produce Change* by Renee Kosiarek
- *Employee LEAPS: Leveraging Engagement by Applying Positive Strategies* by Kevin E. Phillips
- *Feet to the Fire: How to Exemplify and Create the Accountability That Creates Great Companies* by Lorraine A. Moore
- *Deconstructing Management Maxims* by Kevin Wayne

Announcing the Business Expert Press Digital Library

Concise e-books business students need for classroom and research

This book can also be purchased in an e-book collection by your library as

- *a one-time purchase,*
- *that is owned forever,*
- *allows for simultaneous readers,*
- *has no restrictions on printing, and*
- *can be downloaded as PDFs from within the library community.*

Our digital library collections are a great solution to beat the rising cost of textbooks. E-books can be loaded into their course management systems or onto students' e-book readers. The **Business Expert Press** digital libraries are very affordable, with no obligation to buy in future years. For more information, please visit **www.businessexpertpress.com/librarians**. To set up a trial in the United States, please email **sales@businessexpertpress.com**.

www.ingramcontent.com/pod-product-compliance
Lightning Source LLC
Chambersburg PA
CBHW070530200326
41519CB00013B/3002